242

Please Give
a Devotion
for Church Groups

Amy Bolding

BAKER BOOK HOUSE
Grand Rapids, Michigan 49506

ISBN: 0-8010-0623-6

Copyright 1974
by Baker Book House Company

Ninth printing, January 1984

PHOTOLITHOPRINTED BY CUSHING - MALLOY, INC.
ANN ARBOR, MICHIGAN, UNITED STATES OF AMERICA

Dedicated to
AUBREY AND PEARL BOLDING,
two fine Christian neighbors,
who live to help
their friends and relatives

Contents

1

Your Own Back Yard

"Do violence to no man, neither accuse any falsely; and be content with your wages" (Luke 3:14b).

Isn't it great just to be alive in such an age as ours! William Shakespeare said long ago, "The day shall not be up so soon as I, To try the fair adventure of tomorrow."

Isn't it exciting to walk around your garden in early spring? There you see jonquils, tulips, forsythia, hyacinth—all in blossom or about to bud forth and bloom.

If you have no yard of your own, look at the city parks, or the yards you pass going to and from work. All proclaim that there is beauty and growing things.

It is my habit to get up early and walk around in our back yard. My husband asked me one morning why I was getting up so early. "I want to walk around my estate and see about things," I told him.

My estate is a city lot seventy-five feet wide and one hundred and thirty feet long—most of it covered by a house. I think it is grand! Each flower and shrub is dear to me.

The other night a couple came to pick us up and take us to a party. The man got out and began examining my bed of seedum.

"I will get a box and give you some for your yard," I said.

"Oh, no," his wife began to laugh. "We have a nice bed of seedum in our own back yard; he just never goes out to look at it."

Many people are like that. They never look at their own back yard to see the blessings God has given them.

Think of your back yard as your own city, your church, your own house, your family, your own life. You will find that they are better than you think if you will just go out and look.

Like the friend who admired my flower bed, we fail to look at our own blessings. The blessings falling on our friends seem so much better. It just seems human nature to covet what the other fellow has.

Paul, writing to his son in the ministry, realized that he might be tempted to look across at the other person's blessings and be envious, so he admonished him to be content. Wrote Paul to Timothy: "But godliness with contentment is great gain" (I Tim. 6:6). "And having food and raiment let us be therewith content" (v. 8). And in the text at the beginning of this devotion we find Jesus telling the soldiers to be content with their wages.

Remember the story of the prodigal son? He saw the sinful city as something so much nicer and greater than his quiet country life. He forgot for a time how nice it was to have plenty of food and a good home always at his disposal. Defeated, broke, hungry, he came to see his own back yard as a place to be desired and sought.

Our *Lubbock Daily News* carried a story about a local couple who looked at a foreign land and imagined it to be so much better than America. They sold or gave away all their possessions in America. Taking what cash they had, the family traveled to the land they thought would be so grand.

Work was not so plentiful for foreigners there; prices were high, and people were not too friendly. In two years they were back in Lubbock—broke, disillusioned, and discouraged.

Like the prodigal son, home now looked good and beautiful. They found their relatives and friends to be gentle and kind, ready to help them get a fresh start.

Many boys during the Vietnam conflict ran away to Canada rather than fight for their country. After the conflict ended they wanted to come back home. We would save ourselves many heartaches and headaches if we would only look at our own back yards and see the good in them.

In Hebrews 13:5 we read: "Let your conversation be without covetousness; and be content with such things as ye have: for he hath said, I will never leave thee, nor forsake thee."

It may be that you are old or sick and unable to work in your flower or vegetable garden. You still have much for which to be thankful. Remember the days when you were strong and able to enjoy work. Thank God for them. Then look about you. Isn't there much to be thankful for at any age?

Perhaps we are just crawling along on our hands and knees, failing to look up and see the beauty and glory of our own day and age with its great opportunities.

> A tent or a cottage,
>   Why should I care?
> They're building a palace for me over there.

In order really to enjoy and appreciate life at any age, you must have some kind of a goal, a dream, a living Savior.

The kingdom is within you; live worthily.

> When the day has been hard,
>   There's an old-fashioned swing
> In a lovely back yard
>   Which contentment will bring,
>   On a lovely and long summer evening.
>
> Here the sway of the swing
>   Soothes the cares all away
> As its joys gently fling

Out the scars of the day,
    On a lovely and long summer evening.

It is great if you can
    Find a place in your life
Which will serve like a fan
    As it cools inner strife,
        On a lovely and long summer evening.
                                        —J. T. Bolding

2

Post Office Closed

"As cold waters to a thirsty soul, so is good news from a far country" (Prov. 25:25).

"He that sendeth a message by the hand of a fool cutteth off the feet, and drinketh damage" (Prov. 26:6).

During World War II, the post office in our little town was the most popular place in town. Most every home had a connection of some kind with a soldier or sailor fighting for our country. So at eleven A.M. when the mail was brought to the post office from the depot, a crowd gathered.

Messages came each day. Some were good news, some brought sad news, some just news. But there were all types of messages.

As people waited they talked and exchanged the time of day. When the postmaster opened the general delivery window, there was a general rush for boxes or for the waiting line.

Some turned away disappointed, some were happy with expected letters. Some went about town to loiter, others hurried home to take their messages to the rest of the family.

Whatever the news the post office was an important place.

We expected the office to be open for business except on Sundays and holidays.

We might compare the church and its members to a post office sending out messages to all who come to its services.

In John 17:18, we read, "As thou hast sent me into the world, even so have I also sent them into the world."

YOUR MESSAGE
If God's given you a message
    To deliver day by day,
Then He wants it to be given
    In your own especial way.
And no other individual
    Can fulfill His blessed plan,
So it's up to you, my brother
    And it's time that you began.

Someone on you is depending
    For God's truth to help him live,
And you should not fail to help him
    Nor your best refuse to give.
Give him always just the message
    That the Lord intends you to
And then live out an example
    To help get the message through.
                                    —J. T. Bolding

If the church is a post office sending out messages, we must remember that every letter to reach its goal needs an official stamp. The stamps used in a regular post office have the initials U.S.A. or the words United States written on them. Likewise, a messenger going out from the church to take the story of Jesus needs to be stamped with the seal of the Holy Spirit, if he is to be effective.

Our United States postal department has a slogan that goes something like this: Rain or shine, the mail will go. How much more the Christian needs to be positive he will carry the message to those lost and dying.

Some of the saddest stories ever written were about letters that were never delivered and the effects they had on human lives: sweethearts whose letters failed to reach their destination, relatives who lost touch because mail lost its way, positions not obtained because the message failed to go through.

During the depression of 1929, a man had to leave his small-town home and go to a city seeking work. He was successful in finding a position. Each payday he was able to send his family money for living expenses. He knew that in just a few months he would have a mortgage payment to meet on his home. He lived as frugally as possible and was able to buy a money order for the amount needed and mail it to the bank in time. How happy he was when he could write his wife and tell her the payment was on the way.

The sad fact was that the letter never reached the bank and the banker foreclosed the mortgage and ordered the woman and her children to move. People said all kinds of ugly things about the husband.

The poor man managed to get a day off and went home for a visit, expecting to find a happy family. What a homecoming! He found his family at the mercy of relatives and their charity. His home had been put up for sale by the bank. Frantically he rushed to the post office. The postmaster started a trace and a search for the missing letter. The letter was found; it had fallen in a crack.

This story had a happy ending, for the banker was confronted with the money order, dated in plenty of time for the payment. The banker was a man of mercy; besides, property was not selling in such hard times. For a small penalty the banker took the payment and canceled the mortgage. A happy family moved back into their home.

When we fail to take the message of salvation to those who are lost, not always do we get a second chance. Things happen, people are lost by death, at times the Holy Spirit ceases to woo them.

A revival was in progress in a small mining town. The visiting evangelist asked a man to go with him and visit a man

known for his evil ways. The man dreaded the visit and made
an excuse to wait until later in the week. Before that day
came, the man had been killed in an accident deep in the
mine. The Christian was so ashamed for delaying the visit.
The evangelist vowed never again to let a day go by when he
put off telling the story of Christ to someone in need.

The evangelist and the Christian layman closed their post
office for a day and disaster resulted.

It is so important for the message to be delivered each day.

My son-in-law is a rural letter carrier. One Sunday morning
he stopped by the post office on a routine check before going
to church. He discovered a box containing one hundred baby
chickens had been brought in with the morning delivery. The
chicks would die if they were not cared for soon. He took
time (after church) to deliver the chicks, far out in the
country. He did not have to do this, but he felt better
because he knew he helped one of his patrons not to suffer a
loss.

If you close your heart and fail to give the message, you
may cause someone to spend eternity in hell. If your life is
stamped with the Holy Spirit, you will be compelled to keep
the post office of your life open to send the message.

"SEND THOU ME!" VOLUNTEER!

Are there sad and broken hearts that need mending?
Are there near any sick who need tending?
In some lives do the fences need mending?
　　Help me say, my dear Lord, "Send thou me!"

Are there still little lambs that need leading?
Or some hungry ones who may need feeding?
Any hearts with the Gospel need seeding?
　　Lead me Lord to respond, "Send thou me!"

When the young stand in need of thy teaching,
While the message of life still needs preaching,
And the hearts of the lost still need reaching,
　　Help me pray, O dear Lord, "Send thou me."

Are there souls for the Lord that need reaping?
As conviction o'er hearts is now sweeping?
Is there need over sin to be weeping?
  Help me, Lord, now to say, "Send thou me!"
                                    —J. T. Bolding

3

Always a Samaria

"And he must needs go through Samaria" (John 4:4).

"That Christ may dwell in your hearts by faith; that ye, being rooted and grounded in love. . . . And to know the love of Christ, which passeth knowledge, that ye might be filled with all the fulness of God" (Eph. 3:17, 19).

How excited we became when we heard a dear friend of ours was planning to get married. Lots of our young friends are getting married, but this girl is very special. She is past thirty years old and has taught school ever since graduating from college. She always seemed to be helping others and no one ever thought of helping her find a boy friend. God was watching over her and at just the right time He found a companion for her. Suddenly we all began to see how good and kind Sally had always been, how completely unassuming and unselfish.

All the world loves a lover! How often we have heard that statement, and how true it is.

Love is still sacred to most people. Yet there are some Samarias we must see love go through. Love does not always run smoothly.

The disciples did not want to go through the country of Samaria; they had been taught to despise the people there.

Yet they were rooted and grounded in their love for the Master, so they went through Samaria with Him. They even went down into the village to buy food. Christ stayed and waited at the well to win a sinner for the kingdom.

There are people in our nation and our world today whom we have been taught to dislike or to look down upon. Yet the love of Christ is for all. Will we be willing to go through Samaria to win them for the kingdom?

There will always be some Samarias for those who are rooted and grounded in the love of Christ.

Love and giving go hand and hand. A sixteen-year-old boy, Ted, was lazy and irresponsible. One day in the spring a pretty girl looked at him the second time and he was suddenly in love. What a changed person he became! He got a job on Saturdays in order to have more money to spend on the object of his affections. He took pride in dressing up on Sunday afternoons and visiting his new love. He always had some token of his affections to present to the girl.

When we love we do not mind the Samarias we must go through in order to please.

God loves us and so He gives to us. He gives us our blessings day by day: health, food, happiness, joy in service.

In Matthew 7:11 Jesus describes God's gifts to us. "If ye then, being evil, know how to give good gifts unto your children, how much more shall your Father which is in heaven give good things to them that ask him?" Love requires giving, and giving sometimes requires work and sacrifice.

Many of us can remember the days of our childhood when we would answer ads in the magazines for things to sell. There were all kinds of ointments, guaranteed to heal almost any ailment.

Once I sent for some ointment to sell. The company sent me a picture to give away with each box I sold. Well, it was hard work, trudging about the neighborhood selling those boxes of salve. The pictures were so pretty people would buy in order to get the picture.

As I look back over those days more than fifty years ago, I

can see in memory some of those pictures. They were all about love. As a child I didn't realize that; I just thought they were pretty. There was the picture of a mother sitting by the bedside of a sick child, a picture of a huge dog protecting a small baby. One I think we all loved pictured God's care. There were two small children walking near a dangerous cliff, but in the picture an angel hovered over them, keeping them from falling.

God in a sense went through a Samaria when He sent His only son into a wicked world to die for the sins of people. How He must have suffered in heaven as He saw the abuse, the turning away of people from Christ, who came only to give.

A true Christian has a heart filled with love. We do not need to love the wicked deeds of others, but we must see and love a heart that can be changed by belief in Christ.

James was a strong Christian. When he was drafted into the armed services, he found it hard to stand by his convictions. When homesickness, loneliness, and discouragement had almost whipped him, God sent comfort and blessing. James had been the object of funmaking and derision by his squadron mates. Then one day there was a fire in the barracks. Most of the men were still sound asleep. James went to each one and gently shook him awake. As the smoke grew thicker and more dangerous, he came to the last man. This man had been the leader in making James' life miserable. When James saw the man was too drunk to arouse, he started dragging him out. Just as the flimsy roof collapsed, he stumbled with his burden to safety.

Later, when the danger was over, the men all thanked James for arousing them. When sober, his enemy told him he was grateful for his life.

One by one James, through love and patience, won many of his squadron mates to Christ. All learned to admire him; a few became his dear friends.

A young bride often goes through many Samarias when

she must leave her home and go to far away places with her
husband. Yet because her heart is filled with love for her
husband, she goes with him and makes a home wherever they
are.

I admire foreign missionaries a great deal because they
know in advance that they will pass through many Samarias
in the fulfilling of their duties, yet they go on gladly.

Wherever there is life we find Samarias. It is the Christian
who has a companion in Christ to walk through those trials
and show the way.

Hosea is one of the greatest examples of love washing away
hatred in the Bible. Hosea kept forgiving his unfaithful wife.
He spent his money to buy her back from slavery. The love
of Hosea is an example of God's love. We, His children, are so
often unfaithful, yet He forgives and takes us back.

> Sweetly precious and loving's the care of our Lord
>   As He leads in the ways of His will;
> Even though often times it may seem very hard,
>   He attends and provides duty's thrills.
>
> There are times He directs, in His wisdom and care,
>   That we go other ways than our choice.
> So, because of our love we reroute all our plans
>   And give heed to His wish and His voice.
>
> Oh, the blessings that come to our lives when we do,
>   And to those who are hopeless and grim,
> For He leads through Samaria's chill atmosphere
>   That a lost one may come to know Him.
>   —J. T. Bolding

4

Turn on Your Lights

"Let your light so shine before men, that they may see your good works, and glorify your Father which is in heaven" (Matt. 5:16).

> I saw a car the other night,
>   Which I was about to meet,
> Without a sign of a light at all,
>   On a busy city street.
>
> It startled me and my impulse,
>   As I thought of safety "rights,"
> Was to shout to him a strong demand:
>   My friend, turn on your lights.
>
> —J. T. Bolding

We were traveling in the mountains. The scenery was breath-taking. Then suddenly we came to the place where the highway entered a tunnel. A large sign said: Turn your lights on. Without our lights being turned on we could not have safely gone through the tunnel. The way would have been very dark. In just a matter of seconds we were out in the bright sunshine again, but the lights on our car had helped us through a dark place along the way.

Not long after our return home from the trip in the mountains, we were listening to our favorite musical program on radio. The music stopped and the announcer made an urgent plea. "Will all of you please turn on your porch lights. A small child has wandered away from home. The child is retarded and unable to speak well. He loves porch lights and will probably come to someone's porch."

All over the town lights were turned on quickly. People sat quietly listening for a strange sound at their front doors. Our sympathy went out to the parents who were frantically looking for the lost child.

Then the announcer came on with a good word. The little boy had indeed gone to a lighted porch and his parents were on the way to pick him up and return him to the safety of his home.

People began to talk and walk about. Most went to turn off the lights they had so gladly turned on. Most felt a sense of satisfaction in having had just a small part in helping someone in need.

Christ a long time ago looked out on a world dark in sin and sorrow. He saw not just one little boy in need of a welcoming light; He saw countless millions alone, lost and dying, without a light to guide them.

Then He looked across the faces of His followers as they sat on the mountainside and gave them the command: "Let your light so shine before men, that they may see your good works, and glorify your Father which is in heaven."

Despite our lighted cities, our whiteway streets, our cars and planes with bright lights, we still live in a world where we need to let our lights, as Christians, shine. The light of God's love is the only light that will lead men home.

Men today do not need good advice; they need good news.

I heard a missionary speak at a convention. Most of the people were having a good time, showing off their new clothes or bragging to each other about how well the world was treating them.

The missionary looked old-fashioned. Her face had tell-tale signs of much work. Yet she started her message by saying, "I awoke with a song in my heart. My heart is in the sky and my feet are on the ground."

She had a song in her heart because she had given her life to let God's light shine in dark places. If you were the one in darkness and sin, wouldn't you be grateful for someone bringing the light to your heart?

It only takes a flip of the switch to turn on the light for those coming to your home to see the doorway better. It takes a life dedicated to service to let your light shine for others to know your Lord.

Where would our world be today, if those people seated on the mountainside had forgotten the words of Christ and never let their lights shine before men?

> Of what use is a lighthouse without a bright light?
>   A bell buoy without a bell?
> Why have an alarm that will never go off,
>   Or a clock which the time does not tell?
>
> Our Lord's children are saved with the purpose in view
>   That they tell sinful men of their need,
> And then point out God's love offered free to each one
>   Who will trust the dear Savior indeed.
>
> Your lost friends need a hope, and a beacon that's true,
>   An example to guide them aright;
> Let your life overflow with the love of the Lord,
>   And, dear friend, keep a check on your light!
>
>   —J. T. Bolding

5

This Time Tomorrow!

"This is the day which the Lord hath made; we will rejoice and be glad in it" (Ps. 118:24).

"Whereas ye know not what shall be on the morrow. For what is your life? It is even a vapor, that appeareth for a little time, and then vanisheth away" (James 4:14).

> Life is real! Life is earnest!
>   And the grave is not its goal;
> Dust thou art, to dust returnest,
>   Was not spoken of the soul.
>
> —Longfellow

We have no assurance our earthly body will be here tomorrow. We do know our soul will live on forever. Knowing this, for what should we spend time developing and caring?

Once we were planning a trip. It had been some time since we had been on a fishing trip, but now the reservations had been made and our clothes were packed. Another couple planned to go with us. It was hard to wait until Monday, the day we were all to start.

Then the phone rang. My husband's boss was very ill and he would have to take over, perhaps for some time. When he called to tell our friends to cancel our reservations, the man became very angry. To this day he does not understand why my husband could not just pick up and leave, sick boss and all.

Many times we had said, "This time Monday we will be in the mountains." It meant absolutely nothing when duty said you must stay home.

Anticipation is half the joy of a trip, a party, any accomplishment. Yet we must live today if we want to get the most out of life. We really never know what this time tomorrow will bring.

THE LOAFER

He wasted his youth and never would work;
    He thought his life easy and free;
He counted hard labor for those not so smart
    And lazily gazed at the sea.

He tried to imagine a ship would come in;
    Through it, that his life would be made;
But never did he send a ship out to sea,
    So hope could do nothing but fade.

Old age has now come with its host of dire needs,
    Which he cannot work to supply;
Now sick, he still lives on his kin and his friends,
    And bums as his means to get by.

—J. T. Bolding

We live in a fast-moving world. Half a century ago we only dreamed about the "man in the moon." Now we talk glibly about the men who walked on the moon, the pictures we saw, the rocks they brought back for science. We live in a world of tensions, troubles, problems too numerous to mention. We often feel frustrated because there is so little time and so much to do.

Occasionally we read articles about people who have joined meditation groups. They find peace from just sitting and meditating for an hour.

Meditation is nothing new. Christ went aside, evening and morning, to be alone and talk to God in prayer. That is the type of quiet we would all find renewing and refreshing. Does God want us always to be too busy for thought and prayer?

We know not what this time tomorrow will bring, but we can use some basic guidelines to make life a better tomorrow.

The first rule always is TAKE TIME FOR GOD. When we are pushed and hurried, we should stop and ask, IS THIS THE WILL OF GOD?

Always be sure you give a day's work for a day's pay. Then you are eager to start a new day, face a new opportunity. At times look at your life, your daily activities and ask: "Where am I going?"

Face up to the fact if you are going the wrong way, if you are majoring on things that are really minor.

Do not despair and complain when a time of sickness or trouble comes. Without the night we could never see the stars.

Never torture yourself and bother God by asking over and over, "Why?" He knows what is best for His children.

Remember always, life is now, but the soul lives on. Be grateful for the blessings of the past, remember with joy the times you have overcome problems. Repent and ask forgiveness for your mistakes. Above all, remember always, God holds this time tomorrow in His hand.

A young couple just graduated from college started out to seek jobs as school teachers. They were engaged and planned to be married before their teaching positions would start. As they started out that bright spring morning, all the world looked rosy and happy. That night they were brought back to their home town hospital in an ambulance. They had been seriously hurt in an accident. The girl was unconscious for some time. The boy was soon out of the hospital, walking on crutches.

When the young woman at last was released from the hospital, she was not quite herself mentally. The young man asked for his ring back and declared he no longer wanted to be engaged to a girl not quite right.

The girl was very bitter at first. Then as her brain healed and she could think again, she began to be grateful God had spared her from marrying a man who would turn and run at the first sign of trouble. She went to a new town and secured a teaching position. Eventually she met a fine man and married. Her life has been happy and fulfilling. On the other hand, the young man who deserted her while she was hurt and ill made a very unhappy marriage and has drifted from job to job, always looking for some elusive something, found only in stability of character.

> I know not where my path shall lead
>   Through all of my allotted days,
> But this I know, that here below,
>   God wants to guide me through life's maze.
>
> I do not know God's "why's" and "when's,"
>   Nor what each precious day will bring,
> But Him I trust and so I must
>   To His wise mercies daily cling.
>
> So, cling I will, though dark the way
>   And seek to do His will with zest:
> Though I'm unjust, the God I trust
>   Still longs to give His child the best.
>   —J. T. Bolding

6

He Touched Me

"And Jesus, moved with compassion, put forth his hand and touched him, and saith unto him, I will; be thou clean" (Mark 1:41).

In the text above we have the climax to a story. Jesus had been preaching in the synagogues throughout Galilee. He had cast out devils, healed the sick and hopeless. Then a man, an outcast because of the dread disease of leprosy, came and, kneeling down to Jesus, begged for help. He did not ask for food, clothing, or money, only for a touch of the Master's hand.

Jesus did not turn away and say, "You will give me your disease."

He touched him!

What must we do to feel the touch of Jesus?

We must first recognize our need. If the leper had hidden his need, he probably would have died a leper.

After we recognize our need, we must look for a cure. All our resources, whether we are rich or poor, cannot obtain salvation for us from the leprosy of sin.

The poor man in the story saw in Christ a cure. We must recognize in Christ a cure, a forgiveness for our sins.

We, like the leper, must do something about it. He went to Christ and fell down, begging for help. Only when we see our need and fall down asking for help, will we receive the blessing of forgiveness.

In order to ask for help, we must exercise faith.

One spring something seemed wrong with my left leg. Often in the night I would awake with such pain in my leg I would get up and massage it.

I started walking a few blocks each morning before I prepared breakfast. Often it seemed so far back to the house I would lean heavily on a cane. But gradually my leg grew stronger and I could sleep. Why did it grow stronger? I did something about it; I walked.

Jesus touched many men while He was on earth. He touches men now through His children. We are the ones responsible for bringing men to know Christ, to feel His touch of healing.

Not all men respond the same way to the touch of Christ. The leper, against Christ's commandment to "say nothing to any man," went out and began to tell abroad how Christ had healed him.

Remember the ten men Christ healed? Nine went quickly on their way, but one came back to say "Thank you."

In Luke 8:39, we have the reaction of a man from whom Christ had cast demons. The man wanted to go with Jesus wherever He went. But Christ, in His own way, said: "I have a greater task for you. Go to your own home and tell the people there what great things God has done for you."

How true it is today. Christ tells some He touches to go to far away places and spread the Word. Others He tells to go and win the man next door. But rest assured, to all of us He gives a specific task, once He has touched our hearts.

Do you have evidence you have been touched by the Master? If you have, then you are eager to pass that touch on to someone else.

A young woman in Amarillo, Texas, is confined to a wheel

chair because of an accident. She felt bitter and hurt at first. Then from her open hospital door she began to see others being pushed up and down the hall. Most of them were much worse than she felt she was.

The thought came to her one day: service is the rent we pay for the space we occupy in the world.

She started thinking of ways she could be of service from her bed or wheel chair. She turned to the telephone. Now many people each day receive a cheerful call and maybe hear a verse of Scripture quoted. If she reads in the paper of someone somewhere with problems, she writes an encouraging letter.

Every day becomes beautiful for the people who have felt the touch of Jesus.

THIS PRECIOUS DAY

A most beautiful gift from the Lord you receive
    Every morning at break of the day,
As He does in His plan often generously weave
    That again you should wake fresh and gay.

If He opens your eyes on a wonderful world,
    With its blessings abundant and good,
Then before you arise, as in bed you are curled,
    You should ask help to live as you should.

His dear gift of this day He extends unto you,
    But its use you alone can decide;
Will all life richer be as to duty you're true,
    Or will men see its waste and deride?

Let it never be said you're ungrateful at all
    For God's bountiful blessings each day:
May your ear ever hearken to His loving call,
    Then obey Him without a delay.

This good day is God's gift; it will not come again:
    That "each moment is precious" is true;
Therefore live at your best so it won't be in vain
    That He trusted its treasures to you.
                                        —J. T. Bolding

7

No Time Limit on Wishing

"Beloved, I wish above all things that thou mayest prosper and be in health, even as thy soul prospereth" (III John 2).

"Their eyes stand out with fatness: they have more than heart could wish" (Ps. 73:7).

When I think of wishing, I think of my girlhood in Greenville, Texas. Beside our very modest home was a large mesquite tree. Now those trees do not ordinarily grow tall or even very large trunks. But our tree was large. I had a favorite seat where the branches spread out. Perhaps now that tree would not seem so large or so inviting. Then it was a haven from my younger sisters and my brother. How much wishing went through my head as I sat in the tree, reading, dreaming, or just calling out orders to my charges on the ground.

I often wished to make a hundred dollars. That seemed like an immense sum to me at the time. First I would buy a fence; the children would not need watching then. Next I would buy my mother a red dress, because I thought a red dress would show how much I loved her. Then, of course, I would get a chair for the front porch for my dad to sit in. Oh, that hundred dollars would buy so much when I was just wishing.

You might laugh at the wishing a young girl would do, but wishing goes on through all our lives. If you meet a person who never wishes for anything, you have met a person who is dead and hasn't been buried. Or as we used to say, You're dead and don't know it.

In our verse from III John, we find a man of God wishing good for his friends and fellow believers.

In the verse from Psalm 73 we find the psalmist almost envious of the wicked. It seemed that their every wish was granted.

There is no time limit on wishing. There is a time limit on the ability and time we have to make those wishes come true.

If you have good wishes and want to make them come true, you must have courage. In I Samuel 30:6b, we read, "but David encouraged himself in the Lord his God."

David had just seen tragedy. He had returned from battle with his warriors to find their city in ruins, their women and children carried away captive. Verse 4 tells us David and his men wept until they had no more power to weep. Then he encouraged himself in the Lord.

Your dreams will not always come true. Your wishes may seem to crumble around you, but, like David of old, encourage yourself in the Lord.

All America felt sad this year when a young man just a few days away from the time when he would be sworn in as a United States Senator, lost his beautiful young wife and baby daughter in a car wreck.

Don't you know, his dreams crashed about his head. His world became bleak and unhappy. Yet that young man at his swearing-in ceremony held one of his remaining children in his arms and had the other, still too ill to be out of bed, brought to the service by ambulance. He showed supreme courage. He picked up the pieces of his life and went on.

Most people have dreams and wishes, but not all have the courage and ability to face life and go on. It is often so easy just to sit in the tree and wish.

In II Timothy 2:3, Paul told Timothy to endure hardship as a good soldier of Jesus Christ.

A soldier in Vietnam was burdened about the want and suffering he saw among the children. He wished he could do something to help. Then he did help with some of his own salary. He still wished he could do more. He wrote to his pastor in America. The pastor told the church and soon clothing was being collected and sent for the soldier to give away.

The soldier took time to do something about his wishes. People in the churches received a blessing because they could have a part in helping. The poor and needy in Vietnam were helped with things they needed. A good wish come true is a blessing to many people.

DREAMS

I've dreamed many dreams that never came true;
I've seen them vanish at dawn.
But I've realized enough of my dreams, thank God,
That makes me want to dream on.
I've prayed many prayers when no answer came,
Though I've waited patient and long.

Answers have come to enough of my prayers,
That makes me want to pray on.
I've trusted many a friend that failed,
And left me to weep alone,
But I've had enough of my friends that were true,
That makes me want to keep on trusting on.

I've sown many seeds that have fallen by the way,
For the birds to feed upon,
But I've held enough golden sheaves in my hand,
That makes me want to keep on sowing on.

I've drained the cup of disappointment in pain,
I've gone many days without song.
But I've sipped enough nectar from roses of life,
That makes me want to live on.

—Author Unknown

8

Count Your Change in Life

"Even a child is known by his doings, whether his work be pure, and whether it be right" (Prov. 20:11).

"The sluggard will not plow by reason of the cold; therefore shall he beg in harvest, and have nothing" (Prov. 20:4).

Shortchanging is very prevalent among some store clerks. Many money handlers and cashiers make extra money by shortchanging the customers.

Once we have discovered someone giving us wrong change in a store, we are usually careful not to trade with that clerk again.

I want us to think about how many people shortchange themselves.

I knew a man who married the only child of a reasonably wealthy woman. He was not a very good husband and his wife had to work to help keep their home going. Often he spent most of his salary on drink or gambling.

The mother grieved to see her daughter have a hard time and occasionally gave her nice clothes or a piece of furniture. She seldom gave the couple any money.

Then the mother became very ill. For almost a year she was in and out of hospitals. Long before she died, her daughter planned her funeral. The son-in-law often bragged to friends that he planned to quit his job when his wife inherited her mother's property.

At last the mother died and soon after the funeral her lawyer read the will.

Oh, the weeping and wailing, when it was discovered that all her property was left in trust for her grandson when he should reach the age of twenty-five.

There was a small letter enclosed in the papers addressed to the son-in-law. In part it read: You shortchanged yourself when you took pains through the years to be unkind to me. Now I will see that you realize your loss.

On every hand we see people who are too lazy to work; they expect the government to support them. We see it start in school when a child refuses to study and is satisfied just to get by.

In a large family the girls washed the dishes all week. On Sunday it was their brothers' turn. A visitor in the home one Sunday asked why the boys had to wash dishes on Sunday. "Because I want them to appreciate the work their sisters do to keep the home going," the mother replied.

One Thanksgiving the father took all the children to deliver a box of groceries to a very poor family. The father and children arrived at the home about seven o'clock in the evening. They had finished their own dinner and wanted to deliver the basket and get back home in time for a favorite program.

When they were invited in, they noticed the family had been seated around a table with nothing on it except bread and a bowl of beans. The next Sunday one of the boys went to his mother and said: "I'll never complain about washing dishes. We have so many good things to eat. What if we only had bread and beans?"

How often we shortchange our children by failing to make them aware of their blessings and the need of others.

Down on the Brazos River in Texas there were people on

the east bank and people on the west bank. The land on the west bank was good bottom land and the farmers on that side were wealthy. A young man from the east side of the river started courting a girl on the west side. He would row a small boat across the river and walk across the fields to her house.

The girl's father became angry with the young man and ordered him never to come back again. A few days later the boy walked along the east bank and filled his pockets with seed from the dreaded Johnston grass. Then he rowed across to the west side and as he walked across the man's field he scattered the seed.

In just a few months the wealthy farmer died suddenly. His daughter in time married her boy friend. It took the man twenty years and much hard labor to kill out the Johnston grass he had so maliciously planted. He shortchanged himself trying to hurt another. "Whatsoever a man soweth, that shall he also reap" (Gal. 6:7). When you practice shortchange in any form, you are apt to reap the same.

A young lady in college wanted to be popular. She went to all types of parties and soon became known as a girl with loose morals. For a time it did seem that she was a popular young woman, but she had shortchanged herself. None of the other girls would ask her to their homes for a weekend. As college days drew to a close, many of the young women became engaged and were making happy plans. She was one of those left out by boys and girls alike from engagement parties. She had sold out too cheap and lost her schoolmates' respect.

Woodrow Wilson once said: Friendship is the only cement that will ever hold the world together. We all know people who shortchange their friends. When they are together, all is wonderful. When they are apart, they will tell confidences or say ugly things about a friend who trusted them.

Many people think they are shortchanging God. They join a church. When they are asked to help carry their part of the work or financial load, they are too busy or too poor.

People do not shortchange God. They cheat themselves out of so many of the wonderful blessings He wants to pour out upon those who are faithful.

There was an amusing story in the newspaper about a man who snatched the purse of a senior citizen. Two men chased the robber but soon lost sight of him. It just happened that the lady was one of a bus load of oldsters on an outing. The driver of the bus loaded them all back on the bus and started driving around looking for the thief.

Just about the time he decided to give up the chase, he saw the man standing at a bus stop trying to get a ride.

The bus stopped and when the man stepped in the open door the driver closed it quickly behind him. The man still tried to escape when he saw what he had stepped into. Some of the oldsters grabbed him and sat on him until the bus could get to the police station. The small amount of money he had taken from the purse would not even pay his bail.

LIFE

Life was not meant to be lonely,
 Nor yet was it meant to be sad;
There is so much, if we only
 Can see, that will help make us glad.

People are not to be nameless
 Nor like some old dry empty hull;
Life was not meant to be aimless
 Nor yet was it meant to be dull.

Life was not meant to be friendless,
 But full, and of genuine worth;
Nor was it meant to be endless
 Down here on this sin-ridden earth.

So, with our joy in the present,
 And others who travel this way,
That here, and hereafter be pleasant,
 Let's tell of God's love every day.

Oh, but it's wonderful living
  Through each blessed day at our best,
While, with God's help we are giving
  Our lives to be used and be blest.

                                        —J. T. Bolding

9

Silver Trays

"Then I looked on all the works that my hands had wrought, and on the labour that I had laboured to do: and behold, all was vanity and vexation of spirit, and there was no profit under the sun" (Eccles. 2:11).

When my youngest daughter married, she received eight silver serving trays as wedding gifts. She would not need more than one for many years. Her husband was a student and she was teaching school.

"Oh, I do wish they had sent something we need right now!" she lamented.

I thought of a saying I had often heard Mother say when we would make molasses candy. Then we would pull the candy until it was hard. If we ate too much we would become ill. Mother would let us eat and have fun for a period, then she would say, "You can get too much of a good thing."

Some men and women have no higher goals in life than to see how many silver trays they can accumulate, things that are good in small amounts but not worthy of spending a life just getting.

A person is a failure when he has no worthy goal in life.

What would we consider a worthy goal? For a Christian that goal should be to serve the Lord to the best of his ability. There are some people who do not even have the goal of collecting things. They just drift with the current tide. Their only aim seems to be comfortable, to eat and sleep.

I once visited a lady who had over a thousand antique lamps. We could not get her to attend church or Sunday school. She lived to accumulate antiques. Ten years later that woman was a bedridden invalid. When someone did happen to visit her she would complain about never having visitors.

She spent her good years on something, perhaps valuable from a monetary standpoint, but she neglected to give any of herself or her wealth to making the world a better place.

The story of a doctor in North Carolina interested me very much. He wanted to build a hospital for poor people. On the mountains near his office he could see many stones. They were not just something for rain and snow to fall upon. To him they were something he needed to build the hospital. It took him ten years to get the stones brought down to a building site and the hospital built. He had a goal and he kept that goal in sight.

He often asked the patients or their families to bring a stone as they came to get treatment. Many of them took the attitude of a man who said, "If there is joy in going the second mile, think how much fun there must be in going the third." They would bring down a number of stones to the doctor.

Great goals, like great decisions, require great faith. Many people find their life an accumulation of silver trays, beautiful, but useless for so many in every day living.

If your only goal in life is to help someone else up the hill, you will find that after you give them a boost up, you are a little nearer the top yourself.

Mark Twain once wrote: "We are always more anxious to be distinguished for a talent which we do not possess than to be praised for the fifteen which we do possess."

What are the rewards promised to those who spend their lives gathering souls for Christ?

"The fruit of the righteous is a tree of life; and he that winneth souls is wise" (Prov. 11:30).

So the compensations come not in silver trays, or precious antiques, but in spiritual compensations.

Jesus promised us peace of soul—a peace that quiets life's storms. He promised us heavenly treasures, where no robber could steal them. He promised enduement of the Holy Spirit's power. We are the ones who cause power shortages, not the source of the power.

In II Timothy 4:8 we are promised a crown of righteousness. There also are some earthly rewards. Bill was a boy always alone. He just didn't want to be friends with the rougher element in his high school. He felt he did not have nice clothes and spending money to keep up with another group, so he was lonely.

One day there was a special program in the chapel service. A youth director from a local church invited all the students to attend a Friday night program. Bill went and there he met many other young people. Soon he was going regularly and was led to give his heart to Christ. From that day on he had lots of good companionship. No Christian needs to be alone; there is always a task to perform for the Lord: the task of winning someone to Christ.

A favorite verse says, "He that winneth souls is wise."

There was a missionary teacher in Japan before World War II. She started a home for girls from the ages of two to eighteen, who had no place to go. She collected needy children like some women collect china or silver. She had to leave Japan and go back to England during the war. At that time she placed each of her children in Christian homes, hoping to go back and find them when the war was over.

When peace came at last the missionary teacher went back to Japan and was a great help to General Douglas MacArthur in student work because she could speak the Japanese language so well.

When Irene Webster-Smith was eighty years old, she still worked with students in Japan. Her worldly goods consisted of the furniture in a small room and her few clothes. We have not the ability to even imagine the treasures laid up in heaven for a woman who had literally sacrificed her whole life for the girls and boys in Japan.

> So often we do what is pleasing to us
>   Instead of supplying some need,
> And sometimes create such a very big fuss
>   Directing all eyes on our deed.
>
> We major on frills and superfluous things
>   Avoiding the practical work,
> Ignoring that joy comes when somebody sings
>   And not from indulging our quirk.
>
> Our best we should do every day that we live,
>   And never let facts grow too dim
> As we try to supply others' needs as we give,
>   Instead of indulging our whim.
>   —J. T. Bolding

10

Time Out

"Come unto me, all ye that labour and are heavy laden, and I will give you rest" (Matt. 11:28).

"The eternal God is thy refuge, and underneath are the everlasting arms" (Deut. 33:27).

We were attending a college football game. I am not very wise about the way of ball games. At the moment I thought the boys should get in there and push over the line for a touchdown, they called time out.

"Now, why didn't they go on and play while they were all pepped up?" I complained.

"They needed time out to get word from the coach. He signals or tells them what would be best for the next play," my companion told me.

The rest went right on with the game, and in a way I guess I did also, but I started thinking of the many times I personally needed to take time out and talk to my Father in heaven about my problems.

Many games have been won on the athletic field because the players took time out to get the instructions of the coach.

Many lives have been enriched and blessed because people spent time out talking to God.

When my husband was on the battlefield during World War II, I often would grow frantic and think he would never get home again. Each morning after the children were off to school I would take time out to pray. Those moments of quiet time out saved my sanity and gave me courage to keep waiting.

> Dear one who sufferest, take heart again;
> You are not alone in your hours of pain:
> Your Father bends down from His throne above
> To soothe and quiet you with His love.
>
> He leaves you not when the storm is high;
> And you have comfort, for He is nigh.
> Can there be trouble which He doth not share?
> Oh, be at peace, for your Savior will care.
> —Author Unknown

Time out for any Christian is most often a time of prayer. In Luke 11, we find the disciples asking Jesus to teach them to pray.

In just a few verses Jesus gave them a model prayer. About half of the prayer is spent in adoration of the Father. Part is spent asking for God to supply our needs. Very important is the part asking for forgiveness of sins. Then comes the asking for leadership and protection from evil. True time out in prayer will be a seeking of God's will.

In our city there is a popular program called "The Man on the Street." A reporter stops people and asks them questions. One night as I was watching, the reporter stopped a young mother I knew. The young woman and her five children are always to be found in church services on Sunday.

I was eager to hear her answer to the question: Do you approve of the Blue Laws? (Laws saying stores must close on Sunday).

With her head held high the young woman answered, "I certainly do believe in them. If people tried they could buy all they need on Saturday and keep the Sabbath holy."

A few days later I talked with the young woman and told her how proud I was of her answer. She told me she had been harassed some about it. Some had even told her she might be sorry if her husband lost his job over her answer.

From the beginning God planned for man to take time out for rest and communion with Him. Jesus took time to go apart to a quiet place for time out.

A healthy child will run at breakneck speed and play for a few hours, then you will see that same child take a nap or maybe just lie down and look at the sky. He is taking time out.

Men who have a number of employees feel it is important to give them vacation time because they come back to work refreshed and ready to start anew.

Late one Saturday afternoon my doorbell rang as I was about ready to go out. When I answered the door, there stood a little girl with a box of Camp Fire candy. Her lips were blue with cold and her eyes watery with tears. I really didn't have time to spend with her, but I drew her into my warm house and closed the door. When I came back from the bedroom with the money for the candy, I asked her name and address and where she went to church.

She thanked me so much for buying some candy. I knew from the address she gave that few of her neighbors were able to buy Camp Fire candy.

A few days later I learned from a friend that the girl's teen-age brother was in trouble with the law for house breaking. How glad I was I had taken time to brighten the child's life just a little. I really had time to spare after all.

No matter how busy or hurried you are, you can take time out to smile, to say a word of encouragement to others.

During a ball game, often a number of time outs are called. Christians, if they would keep growing and maturing, must take many time outs.

A first-grader went to school one morning without having her hair combed. Her mother was a college student and burdened over her examinations too much to notice what the child looked like.

At school the little girl discovered they were to have their pictures made that day. She went to the teacher's desk and asked her to comb her hair.

"Your mother should have combed your hair!" exclaimed the teacher. "I haven't time to be a teacher and a mother also."

The child went back to her seat and big tears fell from her eyes. No one had time to make her look pretty.

Our Father is not like that. He wants us to declare our love. He wants us to know He loves us. He has all the time there is to listen. We, if we would be happy growing Christians, must take time out.

The Greek word for church means *called-out ones.* If we are called-out ones, we must be people who can take time out for worship.

Some people live a life of being afraid to take time out. Some men are afraid to take a day off from work; someone else might be able to do their job. Some women are afraid to take time out from house cleaning to spend time training their children. We should not be afraid to take some time out for the good things in life.

TIME OUT!

Time out! To speak to God, my coach,
And seek His guiding wisdom for this play,
That on His plan I'll not encroach,
But play life's game in His own precious way.

Time out! To get my breath and rest;
To see the charm and beauty of God's land;
To taste the flavor of life's zest
And recognize His grace from where I stand.

Time out! To watch the sunset and sunrise
And let their glorious beauty, so serene,
Become a benediction of surprise,
Reminding me that God is still supreme.

Time out! As my poor soul bows down
To voice my gratitude again to God,
    And from my face erase this frown
Through thankfulness for sun and sky and sod.

Time out! I dedicate today
My life, with vows renewed; please take the key
    And help me walk thy narrow way.
Time out! dear Lord! But not from serving thee!

—J. T. Bolding

11

What Do You See?

"Having eyes, see ye not? and having ears, hear ye not? and do ye not remember?" (Mark 8:18).

"Thine eyes shall see the king in his beauty: they shall behold the land that is very far off" (Isa. 33:17).

A Japanese student found he was being dismissed from school because he was failing all his courses. He tried to talk to his roommate. The roommate was busy with his own problems. He tried to talk to his teachers but each turned him away with the words, "You should have tried harder. I'm too busy to fool with a failure."

The student dared not go home and tell his parents, they had made great sacrifices to send him to the university. All the boy could see, to end his problems, was suicide. He walked along the edge of the campus, planning how best to carry this out. His life was a failure! That was all he could see. Then he lifted his eyes and saw a sign in the window of a Christian student center. Come in. All are welcome.

He went into the center and found such friendship and warmth as he had never known existed. He found himself telling all his problems to the student director.

When he had finished, the director told him about one who loved him, one who had died for him, one who could help him find a new way of life. He told the youth that Christ would give him strength to tell his parents. The boy gave his heart to Jesus. He saw a new world and new life. He departed to get a job and work. "I am not bright enough for college," he said.

The student went into the Christian center seeing only suicide as a way out. He left with a Savior and friend to give him strength for life.

Part of a song says,

> Open mine eyes, that I may see
> Glimpses of truth Thou hast for me;
> Place in my hands the wonderful key
> That shall unclasp and set me free.

Why do the American people like to travel? Some like to be seen! Others like to travel to see the wonders of unfamiliar places. Many people like to travel in order to meet new people. Friends of mine who own a travel trailer tell me the thing they enjoy most is parking in a trailer court and meeting people from other parts of the country. We might say they see people. They do not see these people as persons to whom they can tell the story of Jesus. No, they see them as people to whom they can tell the story of their own financial success in life.

What do you see? At times we all see ourselves as very small and insignificant. Yet there is a saying: You may be the only light in someone's darkness. What if your light is seen in only a dim fashion?

What do you see? You see what you look for! If you get out of bed cross and find fault with everything, then you see nothing good. If you get up and see the beauty of a white world or the new life of a spring morning, you are glad to be alive and face a day of work.

Do you look at the world and think you are all alone?

Remember you have God. Nothing will ever happen to you that God does not know about.

There was a call for my husband this morning while we were still at the breakfast table. A nurse from a hospital six miles away, wanted him to come and visit a patient. What did I see? The streets coated with snow, slick and dangerous; my husband, retired, yet called every day for visits and funerals.

What did my husband see? He saw a dear friend, old and alone in the hospital. He called his friend's room and talked to him. He told him he could not get to the hospital today because he had a funeral at ten o'clock and another one at two.

What did his friend see? He saw someone still loved him and would be there as soon as he could. When it was time to say good-by, he said, "Brother Bolding, I love you."

What did the widow see when the prophet asked her for bread? She saw only a small portion of meal. God saw the meal replenished over and over as long as there was a need.

A man in our city who had been just a very small-time truck operator at the beginning of World War II was recently asked how he had become successful and rich.

"I saw there was lots to be made if I only thought big and operated on a big scale." He borrowed money and bought a large fleet of trucks. He invested some here and some there in construction, in banking, in pipe lines. In twenty years he was very, very rich, according to Dun and Bradstreet. What changed him into a big-time business man? He looked with a larger vision at the opportunities around.

God gave to His children a gift within—a gift of hope, of security, of love.

Satan wants us to see only fear. He wants us to run from good and see and live with evil.

A beautiful young woman was faced with a problem. She had an offer from a laboratory to work as a scientist. She had the training, she had talent. The job would pay well. She looked at a map of the world. It seemed so large, the places she had never been seemed so many. Should she confine herself to research?

As she looked at the map, she clutched the letter in her hand. How should she answer? It seemed so futile to go and work when she could travel and have fun. Then she seemed to see sick children, old people, youth. She might be able to find a cure for some of their diseases. She looked up to God and said, "I will give myself to the work; other joys may compensate for the lack of travel."

A friend asked a boy she had known all his life why he had left his widowed mother to join a hippie colony.

"Oh, I like to shock people," he smugly told her. He did shock them, not only by his long hair and filthy clothes, but by the fact that he could leave his mother to make a livelihood as best she could.

We who had known him as a willful, selfish child, saw him grown into a foolish, selfish man.

In I Kings we have the story of Elijah promising rain to a drought-stricken nation. He sent his servant to look for a cloud. The servant saw nothing. He was commanded seven times to look for a cloud. At last he reported a cloud the size of a man's hand. Soon the heavens were black with clouds and rain fell.

So many times we look at Scripture and we see nothing. We must read passages over and over to grow in grace and knowledge.

> Some things get lost and I can't see
>   The little vagabonds at all;
> There in the house they have to be,
>   But my old eyes on them won't fall.
>
> I've likely looked straight at them twice
>   And did not see them in each look;
> I must have failed to pay the price
>   Of concentration on their nook.
>
> The chance to be a blessing true
>   So easily can be passed by.

And we can often fail to do
   The good we could, without a try.

Lord, help me make my eyes to see
   What You would have me do each day,
And help me, Lord, that I may be
   A worthwhile servant on life's way.

Lord, help me to behold Thy love,
   Thy constant, providential care;
And as You guide me from above,
   Help me Thy blessings here to share.

                    —J. T. Bolding

12

Monday Morning Quarterback

"I press toward the mark for the prize of the high calling of God in Christ Jesus. Let us therefore, as many as be perfect, be thus minded" (Phil. 3:14, 15).

My husband and I were eating breakfast in a small-town cafe. Along the counter ten men were sitting. It was evident from their dress and familiarity with the waitress that they ate there often.

From our table we could not help hearing their loud conversation. They were discussing the coming football game. Each man had his opinion about how the coach should start the line-up and what plays he should use.

We were strangers passing through, but I am sure if we could have eaten there on Monday morning after the game on Saturday, we would have heard some strong discussions about how many mistakes the coach and players made.

Look at your own life! When problems come, the Monday morning quarterbacks want to tell you how to make your decisions.

A man who had just suffered a great loss opened the door to his pastor with the words, "Don't say a word. Just come in."

Couldn't we often run our affairs better if people just kept quiet?

I had some money, not a large amount, to invest. I had studied and thought about how I would invest it. Then a friend came into the picture. She assured me she had a lawyer who advised her all the time. He had advised her to buy a certain stock. He was sure it would make some money in a short time. I forgot about all the things I had been studying and on her advice went and bought one hundred shares of the stock.

It is now three years later and I am still waiting for the stock to get high enough even to get my money back. That experience certainly taught me to keep my own counsel and never listen to one who is, in effect, just a MONDAY MORN-ING QUARTERBACK.

A young high-school boy wanted to be an architect. He had some talent along that line and felt he would be happy in that type of work. A teacher encouraged him to make plans to enter a school noted for its architectural department when he finished high school. Then along came a fast-talking Mon-day morning quarterback. He told the boy all the hardships of becoming an architect, most of which he just imagined.

After graduation the boy did not know which plan to follow for his life. While he was in a state of indecision, along came a pretty girl and talked him into getting married. So he failed to attend college at all and in a few years with heavy burdens of a family to support he was bitter and rebellious because he had not given himself at least a chance to study architecture.

Be sure when some person is trying to run your life that the person knows what he is talking about. It is best to pray about decisions.

> It's always so easy to pop up and say
> That something was done in an improper way,
>   And some feel so free, from their place in the sun,
>   To ever advise how it should have been done.

If always we thought a bit more than we do
Before we pop off with some spiel near untrue,
    We might in our minds much more tenderly keep
    Concern that our words will not make someone weep.

Dear Lord, grant us grace to be kind and to wait,
Nor ever smart off and incur thoughts of hate,
    Since we may not have enough wisdom to spare,
    And hindsight is easy but foresight is rare.
                       —J. T. Bolding

When we have allowed others to advise and dictate to us until we are in trouble and need help there is a place we can go.

Remember the story of the prodigal son? He had reached the very depth of degradation and sin; his life was a complete failure. Then it was he remembered the one who truly loved him. He said, "I will arise and go to my father."

When we feel there is no place to turn, we too should go to our heavenly Father.

How may I know when a person just likes to give advice and when a person truly loves and cares for me?

Beware of the person who is always finding fault with others but never sees his own mistakes.

Shun the advice of one who slanders those he dislikes.

Avoid listening to the person who shuns work but claims the credit for what others have done.

Every day have convictions of your own and learn why you have those convictions; then stand by them.

Rehoboam, son of Solomon, is a good example of one who listened to untrained advisers. After his father's death he became king. The people asked him to lower their taxes, which were unbearably heavy.

The old men who had been his father's counselors came to him and asked him to follow the wishes of the people. Then he called in young courtiers and asked their advice. They advised him to make the yolk of taxes heavier than ever before.

Following the advice of the young men, Rehoboam sent an insulting answer to the pleas of the people. As a result there followed open rebellion among the tribes. Ten tribes picked a new king; only two tribes remained true to Rehoboam.

He could have been a beloved king, but he chose to follow advice which made him unpopular and lost him most of the great wealth his father had accumulated.

When you follow the wrong advice it is seldom possible to go back and live the play over.

"One today is worth two tomorrows" (an old adage).

13

Life a Two-Way Street

"Upon the first day of the week let every one of you lay by him in store, as God hath prospered him, that there be no gatherings when I come" (I Cor. 16:2).

Life is a two-way street that no man walks entirely alone. Life is beautiful in the proportion we share it with others. We go along taking the beauties of the world for granted until we can't see or have to be shut in; then we long to see them again.

Life is wonderful and happy if we share with others. God, knowing how selfish and alone man would be if left to his own devices, told us to bring of our bounty to the storehouse and share with Him.

Jesus, knowing how unhappy people would be if they tried to walk life's pathways as if they were one-way streets, said: "Except a corn of wheat fall into the ground and die, it abideth alone: but if it die, it bringeth forth much fruit" (John 12:24).

We must die to self before we can bear fruit for the good of all the earth.

A scientist who blesses the world spends long and tiresome hours in a laboratory. An inventor forgets himself as he tries again and again to perfect an invention that will make life easier.

We choose how we will walk on this two-way street of life.

For a number of years now our country has had a rash of young people who wanted to live as if life were a way made for them alone. They defy all the traditions and rules of their parents and country. Why?

I am not capable of saying. I would not judge their parents, for they suffer deeply. I do know those young people have not accepted life as a two-way street. They want only one way and that way theirs.

A two-way street means responsibility! If we do not learn responsibility in childhood and youth, it is hard to live up to when we are adults.

The newspapers carried the story of a man whose skeleton was found in a room. He had been dead about one year. He had walked life's road so completely alone no one missed him for a year. In fact no one missed him at all. A workman repairing a window looked in and saw the skeleton.

The man was not poor; many thousands of dollars worth of securities were found in the room. Yet he was the poorest of the poor in the fact that he walked alone.

Why did I use the quotation about bringing tithes to the storehouse? How can we bring tithes to the storehouse without meeting there with others? How can we be in the church building on Sunday without seeing and having fellowship with others?

When we walk a two-way street our hearts are tender toward others. Often things happen to make us angry or discouraged but we can be more tolerant and pleasant if we have Christ in our hearts.

A couple in South Texas were returning home from the funeral of their only son. They were tired and heart-sick. The son had left a widow and two children. His parents lived more than a hundred miles away.

They decided to stop and eat a small dinner to help them

have strength for the rest of the journey. As they turned into the parking lot, their fender scraped a small scratch on the car next to theirs. They got out and offered to pay for the damages. The other driver started cursing and saying very ugly things to them. At last the couple just walked away into the cafe.

When they came back to their car later, there was a great dent in their fender. Paint on the dent showed it had been put there by the man who had refused their offer of damages to him for a small scratch.

The man failed to remember Scripture: "Be ye kind one to another, tenderhearted, forgiving one another."

There is more to do as we walk a two-way street than merely giving tithes to our church. We must give ourselves to those around us.

A minister told the story of a wife who often asked her husband, "Do you love me?"

The husband grew tired of her question. Finally he told his wife to sit down. He said to her, "I did love you. I do love you and will go on loving you. Now I don't want to hear any more about it."

That husband was not quite willing to walk life as a two-way street. He wanted his wife to go on ministering to his needs each day, but he wanted to deny her the one thing she most wanted to be assured of.

> Some have a share in the beauty,
>   All have a part in the plan,
> So what does it matter—the duty—
>   That falls to the lot of man?
> Someone has molded the plaster,
>   Someone has carried the stone,
> But neither the man nor the master
>   Ever has builded alone.
> Only by pulling together
>   Has man accomplished one thing.
>   —Author Unknown

Walk your two-way street with a smile and a glad word of

cheer. Those on the other side may greet you the same way on a day when you need it most.

A friend of mine works at the state school for retarded children. She says their greatest need seems to be for someone to touch them, someone to hug and kiss them. Then they feel wanted and loved.

She tells me some of the children in that home have not received a letter or a visit from parents in more than two years. Have those parents forgotten that life is a two-way street?

> The cloudy, gloomy, dismal day
> > May tend to bring the "blues"
> And chase away the sunshine gay
> > That brightens rainbow hues.
>
> The somber, dour, sullen face
> > May rob a heart of joy
> And slow its pace in life's hard race
> > Like pebbles slow a toy.
>
> The bitter, harsh, or cutting word
> > The thoughtless often say,
> Great fear has stirred in those who heard
> > And wrecked their happy day.
>
> But smiles will bring a burst of light
> > To those they meet and greet;
> The "blues" take flight and hearts delight
> > When with a smile they meet.
> > > —J. T. Bolding

14

Two Views of Life

"As cold waters to a thirsty soul, so is good news from a far country" (Prov. 25:25).

> Take a pint of ill humor,
> Add one or more unfortunate incidents,
> Set over a good fire.
> When at boiling point, add a tablespoon of temper.
> Baste from time to time with sarcasm.
> Cook until the edges curl.
> Add a handful of haughty words.
> As the mixture curdles, stir furiously and then
> Serve while sizzling!
> Isn't that a swell recipe for a terrible day?
>
> (Used by permission from *Cheer*)

The above recipe has broken more friendships, more homes, more hearts than any recipe you will find in all the cookbooks.

There are two views we may take when we get out of bed in the morning: the view of ill humor, or the view of everything being beautiful. Others cannot choose our view for us; we must plan what we will see each day.

Early this morning our phone rang; there was a death in

the church family. The man was just the age of my husband, his wife a few months younger than I.

My first impulse was, "Oh! how terrible to die so suddenly." Then my view changed. How good that he died suddenly at home. He had not been able to work for a year. A long hospital stay would have left his wife in financial difficulties. So I knew God had chosen the better way to call His child home.

All of life has two views, a good and a bad. We develop our views from day to day.

If you miss something, why be cross and ill? Look for something better to take its place. Parents sometimes miss new clothes or new cars in order to educate their children. They gain the satisfaction of giving their children a bigger advantage than many others.

This is the day and age of surveys. A man made a survey of boys in a poor community. He listed the names of ten boys from eight to twelve years old. He wrote in his notebook the prediction that at least eight of the boys would serve time in jail during the next ten years.

Ten years later he went back to check on his prediction. Some of the boys were teachers, some were storekeepers, some had nine-to-five jobs. He was astounded. How had this come about?

Asking around the community, he was told to go to Grandpa Drake and ask.

Grandpa Drake lived in a run-down house but he had a bright smile and a cheerful greeting.

The visitor showed him the list of names.

"How could they rise above the problems in this community and become useful citizens?" he asked.

"Oh, that is just a small list of names," the old man told him. "I lost my only son many years ago in an accident, so I decided to be a father to all the boys I could find. I didn't feed or clothe them, but I loved every one. If I saw one had a musical talent, I looked for a second-hand instrument and made him welcome to use it. Some liked to saw and hammer, so I turned my garage into a shop. You might say I just loved them."

What did the old man really do? He helped the boys to grow up looking for the good and the happy things in life.

We do not receive a book of instructions with our birth certificate. We are born into this world to make our own choices.

Life does have periods of storm, trouble, and reverses. But on the other hand, there are more periods of challenge, growth, and joy.

How can we help develop the right view of life?

We can keep looking to Jesus. He always has good news for the world, for His children.

At times there is a patch of snow between our back door and the garage door. I send my husband out first and then I step in his footsteps. Jesus went before us and His steps are plain for us to follow.

There are times when we have a sad or discouraged outlook. We cannot avoid these times but we do not have to drop anchor by them and let them become a habit.

Two women get up in the morning. One looks at her house and thinks, I will wash the curtains and clean the floors. I want my family to be proud of their home.

The other one looks at her house and thinks, Let it be in disorder; other women have maids. She acts lazy all day and her family feel no urge to hurry home when day is done.

Two men go out to meet the day. One thinks, Well, eight hours of grind, then I can read the paper and rest.

The other one thinks, I'll work as hard as I can today. My boss is fair and just. When he can promote me he will.

Two views. Each person chooses his view of life.

Some people say, I have no ambition; I will just drift along.

Even a drifting boat goes downstream. If we want to be

useful and happy we must take the view of going forward, of fighting the tides that would pull us back from success.

If we keep looking to Jesus for help, we will read the Bible often. The Bible gives good counsel, good advice, encouragement. Reading the Bible gives us knowledge and strength for daily problems.

A deaf man communicated with his wife by reading her lips. At times when he was displeased or angry, he would turn his back so he could not read her lips. She would shout and say ugly things, but he could not hear her or see her lips with his back turned.

If we look to Jesus for our viewpoint, if we read the Bible often, then we want to say something. We can talk to God by praying. He will not turn His back to us; He will listen patiently and answer our requests.

When we pray and talk to God, we feel a desire to tell others of His love. When we go out to seek and find the lost, then we find our lives happy and useful. We have a great viewpoint of life and its problems.

A family of four lived in a small city. Gradually they grew up and went away from home. The mother and father stayed in the hometown. The father said, "I would not know how to make a living in a different place." The mother said, "It is too late for a move to help my children. I hate this town but my husband is here and I can't leave."

The children married and living in a larger city often longed for the more relaxed days of their childhood. The hometown seemed to them a haven of peace and quiet.

We are responsible for our view of life. Even our health is better if we have a good, a happy view of the life we lead.

IT ALL DEPENDS ON YOU

It's what you see in the world of men
  That makes you what you are;
The good, the bad, the glad, and the sad
  Are scattered near and far.
If evil and bickering, cheating and sin

Are all that your eyes can find,
Then you are as bad as the fellow you scorn,
    For evil is taking your mind.
If you look for the good in your fellow men,
    And help them to rise above
The pettiness there that mars the way,
    And show them the beauty of love,
You'll learn to look through the outer shell
    And search for the heart of gold,
And seeking the good in the world of men
    Will help you your own to mold.
                                    —Author Unknown

15

If You Knew the Blessing!

"If you only knew what God gives, and who it is that is asking you for a drink, you would ask him and he would give you living water" (John 4:10, TLB).

"The Lord still waits for you to come to him, so he can show you his love . . . " (Isa. 30:18, TLB).

A few months after my husband retired, the phone rang one day while he was away from home. The voice of a young lady asked for my husband. After I told her he would not return home until later in the day, she said, "I will ask you one question. Does he still marry people?"

I assured her he was still active along that line. She said that she would call him later.

That young lady felt she had found the answer to all her life's problems. She was happy and excited because she was planning her wedding.

I received a blessing just sharing her joy in the plans she was making. She cannot know, as she plans her wedding, all the joys a long and happy married life will bring. She only knows that to her it seems the happy way.

We cannot know all the blessings God has in store for His children, but we can know they will be greater than we can imagine.

The real fulfillment of life comes not from circumstances around you but from God.

Jesus told the woman at the well that God had a gift for her. He knew how she lived, yet the gift was ready for her when she asked.

An evangelist told of holding a revival in West Texas. The last night a well-built man almost seven feet tall came to him.

"I am large," he said. "I surround myself with large things. I want a large amount of this salvation you preached about." He asked for a great gift and God gave him that gift. We so often live on a small scale of happiness and joy because we fail to realize God has much to give us.

A woman, young and beautiful, but living a life of sin, said to a minister: "Wouldn't it be wonderful if this gift you preach about should really be true?"

If you only knew the gift Christ has to give. We do not receive great blessings because we fail to ask for them. To ask for and receive great gifts, we must set some goals. If we set the wrong goals, we will not receive the great blessings God has to give His children.

If your goals are the wrong ones, you will come to the end of life and have nothing compared to everlasting life.

To have the gift of God's blessings, we must stop not doing, and start planning a course of action.

"Ye have not because ye ask not!"

Why do we hesitate to go to God and ask for the things and blessings we need? Do we let our own sins stand in the way? We have but to ask in repentance and faith and He will forgive our sins. Is it because we lack faith? He is all-powerful. He still works miracles today when they are needed and we ask.

A young woman missionary was home on furlough. Her clothes were the best she could afford, but she looked mousey compared to many of the stylish ladies in the churches where she spoke.

One Sunday evening after she poured her heart out to an

audience about the need on the field where she labored, a prosperous-looking man called her aside. He mentioned the name of a very nice ladies ready-to-wear shop in the town.

"Go there tomorrow and buy yourself a whole new outfit of nice clothes. Tell the manager to charge them to me." He gave her his business card.

Very timidly next morning the missionary sought out the shop. She was amazed at the prices and was very conservative in her selections.

When she went to speak at the same church the next night she felt very proud in all her new clothes. After services the same man came to speak to her.

"Why did you spend such a small amount? I wanted you to have the best. You represent a great cause."

"I was afraid I would spend too much."

"Why, my dear lady, I am a multimillionaire. You could have bought the shop and I would not have missed the money."

We treat God like she treated her benefactor. We are afraid He will not be able to grant all our wishes.

If you only knew what a wonderful gift God has for you!

We cannot possibly ask more than God is able and willing to give us, if it is for good gifts. No parent wants to give a child something that is harmful.

In II Kings 7 we have the story of God's gift to a starving city of people. The prophet Elisha promised the king that on the next day people would be able to buy and sell all the food they wanted.

The king said that even if the windows of heaven opened that could not happen. People were so hungry some had even eaten their children. Yet Elisha knew God was all powerful and he had asked for the blessing of food.

God often uses human instruments to carry out his plans. This time he used four leprous men, outcast from society.

They felt led by hunger to go to the camp of the Syrian enemies. There they found the camp deserted. All the enemy

had fled, leaving behind much food. The lepers went and told
the good news in the city.

> God's great love is so amazing,
>   And His providence so grand:
> Let your heart be filled with praising
>   For the bounty of His hand.
>
> If you only knew the blessing
>   Which the Father has for you,
> And the love which He's expressing:
>   If you only, only knew—
>
> Your amazement would be boundless
>   And your joy would overflow,
> For your doubts would all prove groundless
>   As His love you truly know.
>   —J. T. Bolding

16

Prepare for Easter

"So Christ was once offered to bear the sins of many; and unto them that look for him shall he appear the second time without sin unto salvation" (Heb. 9:28).

A fabric store was crowded with women one spring morning. I was one of the crowd. As we milled about, looking at the gorgeous display of new spring materials, I listened to the comments.

"How will I ever get three dresses made before Easter?"

"Will I be able to match this color in shoes?"

"I wish I had started getting ready for Easter sooner."

Suddenly I knew we were all missing the point. Easter represented the Resurrection of Christ our Lord, not a lot of fancy new clothes.

A few weeks later when Easter came I stood in the church foyer and watched the pretty girls, large and small, as they went in to the services. They were so pretty and so happy. Their mothers were so proud, and some so tired from getting it all together.

The pastor preached a good sermon. His suit was the newest spring fashion, his shoes expensive.

We as a congregation had gotten our clothes ready for

Easter, but what about our hearts? Were we so busy looking at each other we had forgotten to look at the resurrected Christ?

Easter is a glorious time. There is no harm in dressing up to celebrate Easter. The harm comes in forgetting the Christ who arose from the grave.

Easter represents a time of victory—victory over the grave, over the powers of Satan and sin. Christ promised to rise. He always keeps His promises. He promises to give new life to all who accept Him as Savior. Many millions can testify to the fact that He keeps His promise of new life.

When I go to visit my mother in another state, I drive her out to the cemetery where my father is buried. She gets great comfort out of visiting his grave. The headstone is double and she knows that in time she will rest there beside him.

To me that grave is just a place to be kept neat and clean out of respect. My father is not there. What is there is just a worn-out house or body he once dwelled in.

Last summer we visited Jerusalem. We spent some time at the tomb in the garden, said to be the place where Christ was buried. Oh, the joy that came to us as we sang in a service, "Up from the Grave He Arose."

If you are a true Christian, you will mourn the loss of a loved one, of course, but you will be filled with joy as you think of the great Resurrection morning, the day of all days when we will be reunited in glory.

Easter! New life is all about us in nature. We feel new strength in our bodies after the long winter. We need to worship God and feel renewed strength in our spiritual life.

Christ was crucified for our transgressions. He made a sacrifice for our sins. He provided a way of salvation.

When Christ arose from the grave the angel gave a command to His followers. "Go quickly, and tell his disciples" (Matt. 28:7).

That command is still in effect today. We must go and tell. Many years ago, as he thought of Christ and His death for our sins, Isaac Watts wrote:

> Were the whole realm of nature mine,
> That were a present far too small;
> Love so amazing, so divine,
> Demands my soul, my life, my all.

So we come to Easter time. Christ said: "And why take ye thought for raiment? Consider the lilies of the field, how they grow; they toil not, neither do they spin: And yet I say unto you, That even Solomon in all his glory was not arrayed like one of these" (Matt. 6:28-29).

What makes a person truly beautiful? The love of Christ we see in that life.

One spring I went to visit a church I had never attended before. My husband was filling the pulpit for just one Sunday. As is our custom, we went about and spoke to the people coming in to the services.

After the services an old, old woman came up to me and put both arms around me. "Please come back sometime," she said. "I love you." That dear old woman seemed beautiful to me because she was filled with love and kindness.

Easter comes and Easter goes, but the resurrection power of Christ goes on and on, the power to lift sinners from a useless life of sin to a Christian life of service and joy.

A young man was obsessed with the idea he should start a new religion. He went to a pastor and with much zeal told of the new religion he wanted to start. "How would you suggest I go about starting?"

The pastor looked at the young man and replied, "There is only one way to start a new religion. Go out and die for something, get buried, and rise again."

We need not be too critical of the youth. We spend much time getting clothes and such ready for Easter. Get ready by serving the cause of Christ!

What can you tell your lost friends about the Resurrection?

Tell them of the HOPE Christ offers—hope of eternal life.

Tell them of the PEACE Christ gives to His followers.

Tell them of the JOY. There is always joy in service.

Tell them of the SECURITY. Jesus said: "Lo, I am with you always."

Tell them of the SALVATION Christ gives freely.

With Christ as our leader and Lord, how can we be dedicated to defeat? We must be dedicated to victory. He arose! He arose! A victor over death and sin.

EASTER

O the glory of the morning
Of that day so long ago
With its hope of life eternal
  Through Christ's victory o'er our foe.

Hear the glad news as it's spreading
  By disciples on their way;
See rejoicing as they travel
  To their friends throughout the day.

Still the glad news needs our telling;
  Saddened hearts still need the hope;
Tell them Christ has truly risen,
  And in sin they need not grope.

Tell them God will truly save them
  If in Christ they will believe;
Tell them He will give salvation
  If the Saviour they receive.

                                        —J. T. Bolding

17

What Makes a Mother's Day?

"Her children arise up, and call her blessed" (Prov. 31:28).

An old Chinese saying: What makes the greatest joy in life?
The answer: A child going down the road singing, after asking me the way!

Children are said to be the most helpless of all creatures at birth. Someone must feed them, care for them in every way. This duty in a normal situation falls to the mother.

It is the mother's voice the child hears most often. From the mother the child learns to talk, to eat, to walk, and to worship.

To a small baby the mother represents safety, comfort, love, and care. What a privilege to be a mother! As the old Chinese proverb goes, what a joy to show a child the way.

About half a mile from my home there is a large mobile home park. Many little children walk from the camp past our house to a grade school.

As I sit at the breakfast table and watch these children walking by, I can almost tell the little ones who have good mothers. On cold days they will have warm coats and caps on. Some will have lunch boxes.

In warm weather some of the small boys linger in our yard and discuss the flowers with my husband.

Some of these children are in no hurry to walk the long road home. The house will only be empty when they arrive.

Other children hurry by with little bits of handwork clutched tightly to show their mommy. They know she is eagerly waiting for them to arrive.

What makes a mother's day? Is it the glorious day when she holds a newborn child in her arms for the first time? Is it when she sees a child grown up and graduating from school? Is it any day in her life when a child says, I love you, Mom?

It is the father's duty to provide for the family. It is the mother's duty to use that provision well and wisely. It is the duty of both father and mother to make their home a Christian home.

Some women run about and buy all the creams and lotions they can find. They try each new fad in clothes. Their excuse: I want to keep my husband. Creams and clothes are well and good in their place, but the woman who makes a good wife and mother is one who strives for a Christian home.

What makes children arise and call her blessed? A good mother is a good listener. Children and husband need someone who cares enough to listen, someone who will not betray their trust when secrets are told them.

A good mother recognizes that her children have a right to possessions. It is human nature to want some things to be ours. Even small children have this desire for personal property.

A good mother lets her children share in the joys and the sorrows of the family life. In other words, she makes the children feel they are a part of the family unit.

A man I know never seemed to care for prayer or prayer meeting. He attended but took very little active part. Then one day an idea came to him in a crisis. He invited a group of men to come to a tearoom on their coffee break. A nice group came. He explained to them the urgent need of their church. Then he asked certain men to lead in prayer. The meeting became a permanent thing. The men met once a week for thirty minutes, had a cup of coffee together, and prayed together. The man who started the prayer group felt good about it because he thought of the project. He spent time and money to see that it was a success.

A wise mother lets her children try their wings at starting things. She never says, "I told you so," if they fail.

Whatever a good Christian mother does, she sandwiches it in on both sides with love.

There have been many great women in the world—women who are placed alongside the heroines of the world. In the Bible we read of Esther, Deborah, and Mary. In history we read of Joan of Arc, Queen Victoria, Cleopatra, and many more. Yet the women who have contributed most to the good of the world are the countless millions of quiet, self-sacrificing mothers who lived to bring up good God-fearing children and send them out to serve the world.

At a meeting for Cub Scouts one day, some of the boys were misbehaving. One child, large for his age, said, "If they had a mom like mine they would not act that way."

I knew that mom. She was not very large, weighing only about one hundred pounds. Yet her boys were so well behaved. She was not a cruel mom. How did she train them?

After hearing the child's remark, I started observing this little mother more closely. She demanded absolute respect and punished when it was not given. Yet she would sit up far into the night to bake cookies or finish a costume if it was needed for school the next day.

As I knew her better, I found she had dreams of days that would come when she could live more for herself. If she mentioned some future dream she would always end by saying: "But my boys come first until they are grown up."

With all the talk today about liberated women and movements of every kind to get women out of the home, I was amazed to read an article by a famous lady doctor. She stated that she believed the greatest fulfillment would still come for women in marriage and motherhood.

It is true today that a mother does not have to spend long hours over washing and ironing, or even cooking. The modern conveniences have liberated women from much hard work. But nothing will ever liberate a mother from being the best mother she can.

When I was a middle-aged mother with three children in college at one time, you can imagine how much there was left to spend on my own clothes and grooming. I often felt just plain old-fashioned and tacky. On the other hand I had a friend who had no children. She was always the picture of fashion and style. She could go to the beauty shop each week, she could belong to clubs, and go to the city for a shopping spree.

Then the day came when I could go and see my children graduate from college, see them settle into good jobs and later start their families. My life was so rich and so full of exciting things. My poor friend seemed so alone with her clothes and her beauty shop trips. She told me how bored she was with life.

All mothers have influence on their children, good or bad. All mothers must have some courage; it takes courage just to feed and clothe a family. All good mothers make some sacrifices for their children. If they are rich they still need to sacrifice time and effort for their children.

Hannah was one of the mothers in the Old Testament who loved her son very much, yet she was willing to give him to the service of the Lord. Hannah's day came each year when she journeyed to the temple and visited with her son, taking him clothes and gifts.

A returned prisoner-of-war said that the thought of his mother's prayers gave him strength to live during the trying days in prison.

MOTHER'S CROWN
A good mother's crown is her children;
  Her joy is their goodness and grace;
Her pride is their love of the Saviour,
  And peace ever shows in her face.

She counts every day with them precious;
  She trains them to work and to play;
She cares for their needs and their teaching
  And prays for each one on the way.

They soon are all gone from the fireside,
  But memories still are such fun,
And love of a good mother lingers
  In the lives of each daughter and son.
                                        —J. T. Bolding

18

Prepare for Graduation

"The wise shall inherit glory: but shame shall be the promotion of fools" (Prov. 3:35).

"Let not mercy and truth forsake thee: bind them about thy neck; write them upon the table of thine heart: So shalt thou find favour and good understanding in the sight of God and man" (Prov. 3:3, 4).

> Our lives are albums written through
> With good or ill, with false or true;
> And as the blessed angels turn
> The pages of our years,
> God grant they read the good with smiles,
> And blot the ill with tears!
> —John Greenleaf Whittier

So you are about to start a new life! After graduation everything, you think, will be different.

Common sense tells us there will be many new decisions to make. New choices to examine. New tests to face and meet honorably.

Graduation is something you have been preparing for through all the years of your school life. Now that you are face to face with it, are you prepared?

The beautiful mountains you see in your future look blue

and filled with romance from a distance. As you leave your school and go out to climb those mountains, the tests will come.

The first test is about the decision a graduate must make. Who will guide your life, and for whom will you live? Make those two decisions the right way and the mountains in the distance are easier to climb.

Often a new job, maybe in a strange city, will be hard and you will want to give up, quit, go home. Don't give up. If you have chosen to live for Christ, He will walk with you. You may be lonely for those at home but remember you have a friend by your side always.

You are ready to try your wings, to prove you are a trustworthy person, ready for responsibility.

Dr. Brooks, president of the great Baylor University at Waco, Texas, in the late 1920's, sent a message from his death bed in 1931 to the graduating class. In the message he said, "Do not face the future with timidity, nor with fear. Face it boldly, courageously, joyously. Have faith in what it holds." (Copied from a 1931 *Baptist Standard.*)

As you graduate and leave your school, you will be separated from schoolmates. In trying to make new friends in new situations, remember the adage: A man is known by the company he keeps.

As you make and choose new friends, face the test: Is this the kind of a person I want to be known as?

You face graduation thinking, I will be on my own, I can do as I please!

No matter where you go, or how far, if you are a child of God, then you are accountable to God. Remembering this will help you make right decisions.

As you leave the shelter and provision of your parents' home, you will have opportunity to appreciate all they have given you. Your teachers will not seem so mean and out of touch when the knowledge they have implanted comes in handy. Be ever grateful to parents and teachers.

Three daily suggestions to help a graduate succeed in the great freedom of being out of school: Never allow a day to pass without taking time to pray. Be friendly to all you meet. You can never have too many friends. Never miss an opportunity to serve. All service ranks with the boss.

Some of your classmates will be given the opportunity or talent to inaugurate great enterprises or lead movements. To others is given the ability to help and encourage those who lead.

It is only natural as you go out to make a place in the world that you take care of your own interest, but never do so at the expense of your neighbor.

Jackie was a popular girl in school. In college she made friends easily and her grades were average. An unhappy love affair caused her to run away from school. With another girl she went to Europe and spent three months just bumming around. She was classed with the hippies, although she really did not want to be one.

Jackie's parents had spent every penny they could to keep her in the expensive college she attended. They had to borrow money to get her home from Europe and get her to go back and graduate from college.

At graduation Jackie fell into what I call the peril of privilege. She acted as if she were wearing colored glasses and could see nothing except her own desires. Her mother had to go to work to help pay her debts. Jackie abused her privileges as a graduate, as a daughter, as a responsible citizen.

Graduation does bring some privileges. Privileges bring responsibility. Responsibility brings loyalty and courage. To live up to privileges of being on your own, you must have sincerity, perseverance, and determination. Jackie had none of these attributes, so she drifted from one position to another. She wondered why her cousins were all married to nice husbands and she had never had a proposal. She had not learned the greatest lesson of all during her school years, that of looking at others' needs and living for the good of the world rather than for self alone.

CONGRATULATIONS!
You've really made it here at last;
    You've traveled all the way;
What seemed so long has all now passed;
    It's graduation day.

Your happy hopes are now complete;
    Your vict'ry is secure;
You've reached this milestone, oh, so sweet;
    You really did endure.

You are our golden future's hope;
    Its needs you will attend;
We trust you with life's wide, wide scope;
    On you we can depend.

And now we wish you happiness
    As thus you start anew;
May hope and joy of fresh success
    Attend in all you do.
                                    —J. T. Bolding

19

Let Freedom Ring!

"Ye are the salt of the earth: but if the salt have lost his savour, wherewith shall it be salted? it is thenceforth good for nothing, but to be cast out, and to be trodden under foot of men" (Matt. 5:13).

As we come each year to the time when we celebrate the birth of our country, or Independence Day, we feel renewed faith and hope in the future.

On July 4, 1776, the Declaration of Independence was adopted by Congress and read to the people. The United States at that time had only thirteen colonies. What giant men were those who were willing to risk life and freedom for a cause they believed to be right!

The last part of the Declaration of Independence contains an appeal to the Supreme Judge of the world for the rectitude of our intentions. From these words we know the men were God-fearing and depending on God for help in the new country.

How God has protected and cared for the United States of America, during the years since that group met in the Independence Hall at Philadelphia! How many blessings and gifts He has poured out to our country.

We have a heritage that is truly great and glorious. We must be faithful to teach our children about the heritage of freedom, freedom won by blood and sweat and tears. Our road is smoother and easier to travel because others went before us. Our forefathers held the flag of their country high and treasured freedom with their lives. Let us be willing to fight that our flag may always fly free and beautiful over our land.

Benjamin Franklin said, "I have not yet, indeed, thought of a remedy for luxury." Have we as a nation grown so used to luxury we lose sight of the foundation upon which that luxury was obtained?

In the living room of a very successful business man's home a few days ago, we were discussing the fuel shortage.

"Americans are ingenious, and inventive," he said. "I have no fear but that they will find a way to make new kinds of fuel and energy."

Such confidence has helped our nation to develop.

I like the story about the girls in a small village in the East because it illustrates in a small way how our great country has developed industry to meet needs.

A man from the village ran a boat back and forth between the village and Philadelphia. A lady in the city owed him for some services for which he refused to take pay. She, knowing he had a teen-age daughter, sent a present of a new-fashioned cap to the daughter. Needless to say all the girls in the village wanted a cap like that of the skipper's daughter.

In a few months all the girls in the village had such a cap. How? The girls all knew how to knit. They made mittens and sent them for sale in Philadelphia. For the mittens, the skipper brought back ribbons and laces so each girl could make a cap.

Such industry did not die with the eighteenth century. For the past few years in our city it seems that everyone has been determined to take a trip abroad. One of my friends, a school teacher, determined to go. Her husband refused to give her the money. She went anyway. Nights she worked crocheting wool purses. She sold the purses to a local department store. By the time the tour left for Europe she had the money to go.

I am not saying I approved of her going against her husband's wishes. I only want you to see how we work and plan ways to get what we want. That has been the American way; that is a mark of independence.

Think for a moment about spiritual freedom. Can we have true freedom in government if we fail to have freedom in our spiritual lives?

Jesus said, "Ye shall know the truth and the truth shall make you free."

What is the truth?

If we are to have a great nation we must rely upon God. If we rely upon God we will try to follow His commandments. We will believe in Christ, the Savior of the world.

In the Ten Commandments, God gave Moses the basis for laws to govern a nation, a people. Even today those laws will make a great basis for a nation to be governed by.

What good will we reap while we lead the world in scientific advancement if we let Satan place our souls in bondage? There is no advantage in the tallest buildings, the most advanced schools, the best-fed people, if we leave our souls in the bondage of sin.

We are on this earth a few years at the most; we will be in eternity forever. Are we willing to work for a divine reward in a heavenly home?

If Christ is not honored by our nation, then the government will be run by power-hungry men who can turn into tyrants.

"For unto us a child is born, unto us a son is given: and the government shall be upon his shoulder: and his name shall be called Wonderful, Counsellor, The mighty God, The everlasting Father, The Prince of Peace" (Isa. 9:6).

We Americans must trust in Christ if we would let freedom ring in our land.

I am so thankful for this land,
  With glorious heritage so dear,
And courage of our forebears grand,
  Who labored hard their fields to clear.

I'm grateful for the fertile soil,
  Which bears good harvests year by year,
And for the minerals, coal and oil:
  Resources which God planted here.

For mountains, plains, and forests tall;
  For cities great, and honored law;
For homes, and schools, and children small,
  With gratitude, I stand in awe.

In this great nation, wide and free,
  My life is lived in joy and peace;
And this my prayer shall always be
  That its sweet freedom never cease.

This is my own, beloved land.
  So dear and wonderful to me;
Of all I've seen, it is most grand;
  My best I'll give to keep it free.
                                        —J. T. Bolding

20

A Handful of New Days

"The Lord sitteth upon the flood; yea, the Lord sitteth King for ever" (Ps. 29:10).

When I was young, New Year's Eve meant a party and lots of fun. It usually was a church-sponsored party. At twelve o'clock, we would all stand in a circle holding hands and singing "Blest Be the Tie that Binds." We would thank our sponsors and go home to spend the rest of the night sleeping.

Now I am many years older. New Year's means another year of my life has gone by like a rushing flood, stopping for nothing, for no one.

Each new year I wonder what will happen in our world these next twelve months. What will happen to my family, my friends, to me?

Holding out my hand, in imagination, I see a handful of new days. How many will be mine, I do not know. Only the Lord who sitteth upon the flood of life and time knows.

As a freckled teen-ager, laughing and holding hands as I sang, how little I dreamed of the changes our world would see in the next fifty years.

In my wildest imagination I did not dare to think of a time when men would walk on the moon. The moon! So far away, so dreamlike in quality to youth in the Twenties.

Riding in a Model T or in a train, how could I know the floods of time would let me see my friends flying across the nation, the world, in fast planes? How could I know I would see things happening thousands of miles away, just as they happen, by means of television?

Life was so simple then. My most serious problem was wondering if I would make good grades in school or get a new dress for a special occasion.

Now with our world in turmoil, I must stop often throughout the day and remember: the Lord sitteth upon the flood.

Remember, He is the one sure and steadfast anchor as the floods of crime, sorrow, inventions swirl about us.

One Spring day in 1938 we started out for our church north of Dallas. Heavy rains had flooded the lowlands along the Trinity River. Before we realized it, we came to a place where the water covered the highway.

In those days, people had time to help each other. Two teen-age boys had their overalls rolled up above their knees. They thought it great fun to walk across the flooded area by the side of the cars. With bare feet and long sticks, they guided the driver, keeping him on the pavement which no one could see but which they could feel.

"Keep looking at the far side, don't look at the water and get frightened," they would advise each driver.

My husband was a careful driver, but I was very frightened. Our three small children were in the back seat. If we were to be washed off the road into deep water we would all be drowned.

Once we had started across there was no turning back. We must trust our lives to the guidance of the barefoot boys with their long wooden sticks.

So we face each new year. We must trust the one who gives us a handful of days, then controls the floods which swirl around us. He will guide us with all power and knowledge.

Can you imagine what we did when we reached the higher ground on the highway and could see the pavement? We said, "Oh, thank you, God."

As we come to a new year, knowing the old is out of our hands, do we stop and say, "Oh, thank you, God, for bringing us safely through our troubles and trials"?

If I bake a cake I expect it to be good when I take it out of the oven. Why? I have followed the recipe; I have used the best ingredients possible; it has everything to make it good.

With this handful of days, given us to use as we will, we must expect them to be good and useful.

If we start the year with bitterness, jealousy, hate, ill-will, we will not have a good year. We are not starting with a clean heart. Our ingredients are all wrong. Better to fill our handful of days with faith, hope, love.

A bachelor cowboy once bought a cookbook. Later the lady who sold him the book asked, "Have you baked anything good yet from the cookbook?"

"No, ma'am," he replied. "I never tried. The first line said, 'Take a clean vessel.' I didn't have a clean vessel and I didn't want to wash dishes."

Just a joke! But how often we fail to have a bright new year because we will not clean out the impurities from our hearts and lives.

"Delight thyself also in the Lord; and he shall give thee the desires of thine heart" (Ps. 37:4).

> I look backward,
> I look forward,
> What do I see?
> An old year gone
> With tears and joy,
> A new year out before me.

One by one your handful of days will slip from your fingers. They will go into eternity's vast domain. They will never come again to be lived and used for God's glory and your good.

Today is not just another day; it is *this* day! A day to be lived and used in such a way that you will not later look back and sadly say, "If only I had used my time in a different way!"

A day wasted is such a sad thing. We cannot call it back. We must in time give an account for it to the one who controls the floods of life and time.

As I face a new year, I know my life is a journey nearing the end of the road. Yet I plan to take my handful of days and, like David in Psalm 23:4, I will fear no evil.

Remembering Ephesians 4:32, I will be kind, tender-hearted, forgiving to others.

As Paul admonishes in I Corinthians 16:13, I will stand fast in the faith.

Remembering Joshua 1:9, I will be strong and of good courage, I will not be afraid, for my God will be with me.

When this handful of days has drifted through my fingers one by one, I hope to give a good account of my time and talents and look with joy for the coming of my Lord.

THE NEW YEAR

Come let us anew
Our journey pursue,—
Roll round with the year,
And never stand still till the Master
appear;
His adorable will
Let us gladly fulfil,
And our talents improve
By the patience of hope, and the labor of love.

Our life is a dream;
Our time, as a stream,
Glides swiftly away,
And the fugitive moment refuses to stay:
The arrow is flown;
The moment is gone;
The millennial year
Rushes on to our view, and eternity's near.

Oh, that each in the day
Of His coming may say,
"I have fought my way through;
I have finished the work thou didst
give me to do";

Oh, that each from his Lord
May receive the glad word,
"Well and faithfully done;
Enter into my joy, and sit down on my throne."

—Charles Wesley

21

What Makes Christmas?

"And again, when he bringeth in the first begotten into the world, he saith, And let all the angels of God worship him" (Heb. 1:6).

"Behold, I bring you good tidings of great joy, which shall be to all people. For unto you is born this day in the city of David a Saviour, which is Christ the Lord" (Luke 2:10, 11).

What makes Christmas? Is it holly and snow, a lighted tree in the firelight glow?

Is it the beautiful songs we love to hear? "Joy to the World," "O Little Town of Bethlehem," "Hark, the Herald Angels Sing." These and many more thrill and bless our hearts at Christmastime.

The decorations, the songs, the gifts should all remind us of the prophet's admonition to the angels, to worship Him.

What makes Christmas?

The wise men of old said, "We have seen his star" (Matt. 2:2). After seeing the star, they went to seek Christ and to worship Him.

Sometimes we get so excited about all the glitter and glow of Christmastime, we forget which star to seek.

Christ was born into a dark world. Men went about with

small torches or lamps burning oil. Yet Christ brought a great
light, a light to shed its beams to the farthest corner of the
world, even, as we know now, to the surface of the moon.

Christ was born into a poor world, yet He brought the
greatest riches man can know, giving them as a free gift to all
who would accept Him.

Is it any wonder we think of Christmas in connection with
love and gifts to those we love! Christ set the example.

One Christmas a man in Chicago decided to try an experi-
ment in gift giving. He went to his bank and drew out a
hundred dollar bills. Then he went to a very busy street
corner and started holding out dollar bills to the people
passing by.

Most of the people just walked a little faster, fearing he
was a madman. Some laughed and said comic things like,
"You keep it, fellow. You need it for a doctor."

Two small paperboys came to the corner. They were tired,
hungry, and cold. When they saw the man holding out his
dollar bills, they ran up to him, holding out grimy hands to
receive the gift. After each had received a bill, one boy asked,
"Now what do you want us to do to earn this money?"

"Not one thing; just have a happy Christmas."

How Christ longs for us to accept the gift of salvation from
His outstretched hands. He does not ask us to earn or work
for it, only to believe and accept. Then we will want to serve
and worship Him.

What makes Christmas? God made it by giving. We celebrate it by giving.

A second-grade teacher was amazed at the things her small
pupils found to complain about. One night while reading the
paper she saw an appeal for people in America to adopt
refugee children in Formosa, from mainland China. As a
result her second-grade class decided to adopt a seven-year-
old girl.

The project was very exciting to the children. They talked
about their Chinese sister. The children ran errands and

helped in any way they could to raise the small amount of money needed to keep the girl in a mission school.

From time to time the missionary sent letters and pictures of Chen Ke Wei. The second graders became much more thankful for their nice homes and school.

What makes Christmas? To really know we must know Christ. To know Him is to love. When we love Christ, we love even the most needy and helpless.

What makes Christmas? Forgetting! Never thinking about what others can do for you. Thinking how you can help spread the knowledge of salvation. Love is giving, forgetting self, helping others.

The Pittsburgh, Pennsylvania, newspaper told the story of a blind school teacher, unmarried, yet longing for a child. After much legal red tape, Miss Claypool adopted a blind girl, three years old. When she came to live with her new mother, the child could crawl with difficulty, could only speak a few words. With the love and care lavished upon her by her new mother, she could soon walk and talk as well as any other three-year-old.

What did the teacher get in return? The care and responsibility of a small child. The love of one who often said, "I love you, I am yours."

God saw our needy world, longed for us to grow and develop into better people. He adopted us at the great price of sending His begotten son into our world to die for us.

What makes Christmas? Is it the way we celebrate the day?

I'M READY

I'm ready for Christmas, said dear little Jane
With a smile on her face, so sweet and plain.
I have just peeped under Grandmother's tree.
I know there must be a gift there for me.

My gifts are all wrapped and ready to give.
An apron for Mommy, a thimble for Sue.
Dad needs some slippers, and I got those too.
There is even a gift for baby just three.

Oh, I wish I knew what they have for me—
　"Come, Jane, and ride over town with me,
I'd like you some poor little children to see."
　The voice spoke soft and lo, but Jane arose and
　　was ready to go.

She saw little girls without any shoes,
　And poor little boys with no toys at all.
They seemed to be hungry, their bodies were so small.
Jane said, "Oh, God, I don't need any gifts at all."

The Wise Men made their first Christmas great by opening their treasures and offering them as gifts to the Christ child.

There is not a person in the world who does not have some treasure to give the Christ child. Every person has a life, some black with sin, some young and innocent. Christ wants each one.

A first-grade boy, Dan, lived in a trailer park. He loved his teacher very much. The long walk to school each day did not bother him; he knew there would be a smile and an encouraging word when he arrived.

As Christmas drew near, the children began to talk about what they would give the teacher. It seemed to Dan they must all be rich; he knew of no gift he could bring.

As time for the Christmas party at school drew near, Dan became withdrawn and sad. He felt so ashamed to have no gift for his beloved teacher.

As Dan walked to school the morning of the party, he found a stray kitten someone had abandoned near the highway. Dan picked up the half-frozen kitten and held it under his coat.

As Dan trudged along he began to dream about how nice it would be to have a pet kitten. He had always wanted some box to sleep in near his bed.

When Dan went into the school room, he still held the cat under his coat so he sat down with coat on.

There on the teacher's desk he saw gaily wrapped packages from the other pupils. Looking at his teacher, he knew he must give her something. He walked to the teacher's desk and removed the kitten from its warm refuge.

"Here is my kitten for your Christmas gift." He held out his new-found treasure.

"Why, Dan, how sweet of you!" The teacher took the cat for a moment. "I tell you what. I am gone from home so much. Will you keep this kitten for me?"

"Oh, yes, ma'am!" Dan returned to his seat happy and pleased that his gift had been accepted.

Jesus keeps our lives when we give them to Him, yet He trusts them to our care for growth in grace and knowledge.

I have a treasure to give, my life. You have a treasure to give, your life. That makes Christmas.

CHRISTMAS
Let happiness replace our scorn,
And Christlikeness our lives adorn:
This is the time when Christ was born;
   It's Christmas time again.

The time of giving gifts is here;
Our streets and homes are filled with cheer,
And God seems very, very near;
   It's Christmas time again.

Rejoicing overflows our hearts,
While kinder words replace sharp darts,
And Mother fills the grocery carts;
   For Christmas feasts again.

And so we thank God for His Son,
For all the wond'rous things He's done
And for His love that leaves out none;
   It's Christmas time again.
          —J. T. Bolding

22

Thanksgiving

"Rejoice evermore. Pray without ceasing. In every thing give thanks: for this is the will of God in Christ Jesus concerning you" (I Thess. 5:16, 17, 18).

Thanksgiving is something so big we cannot put it in the month of November and tie it with a bow. Thanksgiving is something so wonderful we must open the package and let it fill the atmosphere of our whole year.

Our youngest daughter has been married fourteen years and lives in California. During these fourteen years we have never been with her at Thanksgiving time. This year we decided to make a trip at Thanksgiving and spend the time with her.

When she heard, she called to tell us how welcome we would be. "It has always been such a sad, lonely day for us so far from home."

Then the thought came to me of the first Thanksgiving, more than 350 years ago. The people planned a day of Thanksgiving. They were not only far from home, but most of them knew they would never be able to see their homeland again. Yet they were thankful.

How many here will sit down to a feast on Thanksgiving

Day and before the meal is over be complaining about the food not being quite perfect, or the weather being bad!

Each person has a charge to keep about Thanksgiving. Paul said, "In every thing give thanks."

So, first give thanks to God. He is the giver of every good gift. When you have given thanks to God, as day follows night, you will want to express gratitude to someone else.

Last week we made detours in our neighborhood in order to drive by some beautiful trees. Trees in West Texas are not plentiful, and trees covered with beautiful red leaves are rare. We did not plant the trees we drove by to see. We did not spend a penny watering or fertilizing them, yet we were blessed with their beauty.

You may be thinking: I have no trees or flowers to share. You have some beautiful kind words and you may share them with others any day. Call someone you know who might be sad or alone and just let him know you are thinking of him. Offer sympathy to someone who has recently experienced a death in the family.

You will enjoy Thanksgiving better if you plan each day to share joy with others.

I was touched by a story in the newspaper a few years ago about a boy in Indiana. The Governor of the state heard about a boy just sixteen years of age, in prison for robbery. When the Governor looked into the case he found the boy's father had terminal cancer. The boy had been driven to steal because of the desperate plight of his family.

On Wednesday before Thanksgiving the boy was given a pardon and sent home to his family. How grateful that young boy must have been to his governor.

Our heavenly Father looked at us in the prison of our sin and sent His only Son to offer us a way of pardon and forgiveness.

One day at noon a family was saying cross things to each other. Some of the children were cross because they could not have an outing they had planned on. The mother was cross because she was tired and overworked. The father just felt he shouldn't be expected to work around the house so much on Saturday.

As they were about halfway through eating, the postman came. One of the smaller children ran to get the mail. There was only one small letter, addressed to the whole family.

The father opened the letter. It was a thank you note from a lady down the street. It read:

"Thank all of you for letting my little Billy play in your yard last Saturday. We are new here and he has been very homesick for his old friends.

"You are welcome to come to our yard and play anytime. We are glad to have such nice neighbors.

Sincerely yours,
Mrs. Bowen"

"Wasn't that nice?" the mother exclaimed.

"Mother, let us go today. They have a large tree to climb," one of the children said.

Soon the whole family seemed happy and was making plans for a happy day.

Send a thank you note today to someone you have neglected.

Thanksgiving is a way of life. It must be practiced and given to others if you would be truly happy.

For many years my husband gave pieces of chewing gum to the little children after church. The chewing gum helped them wait a little longer for lunch. Giving it helped him feel he had made someone a little happier for a few moments. At times when my grocery bill seemed larger because of the many packages of gum, I would complain a little. Then one Sunday I saw a little girl about nine years of age run down the hall to catch my husband. He had just given away his last piece of gum.

Putting his arm around her, he sadly said, "I haven't any gum left today."

"Oh, I don't care. I just wanted to see you." She walked along in the circle of his arm, talking about her class and her teacher.

Following along behind, I noticed she was all alone. At the church door she said good-by and took up her post to wait for someone to come from her home and pick her up. Perhaps her little visit with an older man who loved children was the bright spot in her day. After that I always tried to see happy children as I bought gum on grocery day. He was not just giving gum away; he was giving himself away.

WE GIVE OUR THANKS

It's the time of our nation's Thanksgiving again,
The glad season when harvests are all gathered in,
When we count up our wonderful blessings and then
    Make a point of expressing our genuine thanks.

All the harvests surveyed, we then turn to our health.
Then we number our homes and our families as wealth;
Opportunities dear, not enjoyed by our stealth:
    So we offer expressions of genuine thanks.

For sweet freedom to worship our own special way;
For our friends and the wonderful things that they say;
For the mountains and valleys, all nature array:
    We so joyfully give our most genuine thanks.

Every God-given day is a treasure indeed
And the blessings of each ought our gratitude speed
Until deep in each heart it is surely agreed
    Every day is the time for our genuine thanks.

                          —J. T. Bolding

23

A Bountiful Harvest

"Oh that men would praise the Lord for his goodness, and for his wonderful works to the children of men!" (Ps. 107:8).

A small group of men formed the habit of meeting before work for prayer. They were praying for their sons who were in the armed forces during the Vietnam conflict. Two of the young men were prisoners of war.

Then the day came when the war was over. The prisoners were released, the men in service being moved home or to other places.

People all over our nation were touched and jubilant. One man went to the place of prayer that morning. He stayed a few moments and then left for work. As he left he met one of the other men who had been faithful to the prayer group through the months.

"Why did you come to pray today? The boys are safe now."

"I came to thank God that our prayers have not been in vain. They have been answered."

Few people cultivate the art of being thankful, yet the ones who do are the truly happy people.

One of the prayer group members who prayed for the boys

to return, complained constantly because his son was thin and undernourished. He failed to be thankful that his son had managed to survive the suffering and starvation of prison camp.

Those who truly reap a bountiful harvest in life are the people who are grateful for each blessing, large or small.

"Thou crownest the year with thy goodness; and thy paths drop fatness" (Ps. 65:11).

It was said of the old Tartar hordes that grass could grow no more where their horses had traveled. Not so with the wonder of God. Wherever God travels there is goodness and plenty.

THANKFUL

Fields have born their golden harvest,
Autumn blossoms cover hill crests
    At this glad Thanksgiving time.
Forest trees lift up their branches,
    Decked in gold and red and brown;
Mountains, valleys, farms, and ranches
    Bask in sunshine's halo crown,
        At this glad Thanksgiving time.

Underneath the church house steeple
Gather many thankful people
    On this glad Thanksgiving Day.
And they sing their grateful praises
    For rich harvests from the sod
As the congregation raises
    Songs of gratitude to God
        On this glad Thanksgiving Day.

—J. T. Bolding

A bountiful harvest at Thanksgiving comes when we have grateful hearts, when we can open our mind's eye and see our blessings.

One evening we spent a pleasant hour with friends eating ice cream. After we returned home I had a terrible headache. Nothing we did seemed to ease the pain. Finally I tried to be very still and make my husband think I was easy and asleep. I knew he had been working all day and needed his rest. As I suffered far into the night, the thought kept coming to me, Will I be alive in the morning?

Finally I did drop off to a restless sleep. The next morning I was so grateful to God for life. The sun was shining and the flowers were blooming. How thankful I was to be breathing and able to get up and prepare breakfast.

As I thought of the horrible night of suffering, I thought of the blessed release of rest at last. It is great to thank God for life. It is wonderful to thank Him for rest that renews our strength.

My friend Aillene had been in the hospital for ten days. The day she returned home, friends brought in food, cooked and ready to serve. The next day more friends brought food and dusted her house. She was so weak and tired all she could say was, "Thank you." Later she said she thanked God over and over for friends.

There can be no bountiful harvest of friends unless we sow the seeds of friendship.

In recent years there have been many workers who have gone on strikes. Some strikes have accomplished their goal; others have caused only hardship and sorrow.

Mr. Elwood worked for a steel company. Because he had a large family he had not been able to save very much for rainy days. When the workers in his company went on strike, he saw no way to keep his family fed and the bills paid. He began to pray for God to help him. As God always does, He answered the prayer. The oldest boy, Tim, was able to get a paper route. The daughter found an old woman who needed a companion at night. She was glad to help out. Mr. Elwood himself found some odd jobs to help tide things over.

The first meal the family had together after the strike ended, Mr. Elwood prayed, "Thank you, God, for a chance to work."

Work is a blessing and we should be grateful for the strength and privilege of work.

We lose such a great harvest of blessings when we fail to be thankful for the many little unremembered things which all add up to make life happy and beautiful. The laughter of children, the beauty of the full moon, the first wild flowers in spring. So many things we take for granted, yet we should be so thankful for each one.

We went to an open house given by high-school boys from the poorest part of the city. Under the supervision of their teacher they had built a nice three-bedroom house. As our guide took us over the house, he proudly pointed to the part he had taken in the construction. The house was very attractive and the boys seemed so grateful for the opportunity they had to build it.

Realizing from what section of the city the boys came, we knew many of them had never been in a house that nice before.

"The work on that house will inspire those boys to go out in life and work for similar homes," my husband remarked.

At least we were well aware of how grateful the boys were for the opportunity of learning how to build something.

Your harvest of blessings depends upon you, how you sow the seeds of thankfulness and helpfulness throughout the year.

MY THANKSGIVING

I offer thanks for just familiar things;
The ruddy glow of the sunset sky,
The shine of firelight as the dusk draws nigh,
The cheerful song my little kettle sings;

The sense of rest that home so surely brings,
The books that wait my pleasure, true and fine,
Old friendships that I joy to feel are mine.
I offer thanks for just familiar things!
—Author Unknown